ADVANCE PRAISE FOR
Veggie BURGERS EVERY WHICH WAY

"THIS IS A TERRIFIC BOOK! I've never been a fan of veggie burgers—neither the word 'veggie' nor the dry little disks with their strange little flavors. But Lukas Volger has just the right idea: Make real food with real flavor—and burgers that go far beyond any microwavable snack. There's a lot to like in *Veggie Burgers Every Which Way*, including some very appealing sides, dressings, and, what else? Buns! I'm headed to my kitchen right now."

—DEBORAH MADISON, author of *Vegetarian Cooking for Everyone*
and *Vegetarian Suppers from Deborah Madison's Kitchen*

❋

"LUKAS VOLGER'S BURGERS are made with real food—fresh produce, whole grains and beans, fresh herbs and spices—combined with imagination and great taste. This appealing book is the best collection of vegetarian burgers I've ever seen, a refreshing departure from the overprocessed veggie burgers of yore."

—MARTHA ROSE SHULMAN, Recipes for Health, nytimes.com
and author of *Mediterranean Harvest*

❋

"THE WORLD OF BURGERS has just grown bigger, fresher, more colorful, and deliciously diverse thanks to Lukas Volger's back-to-basics approach to the veggie burger. Summer barbecues may never look the same again!"

—CATHY ERWAY, author of *The Art of Eating In* and NotEatingOutinNY.com

THE EXPERIMENT BECAUSE EVERY BOOK IS A TEST OF NEW IDEAS

veggie
BURGERS
EVERY WHICH WAY

FRESH, FLAVOR-
FUL, HEALTHY VEG-
ETARIAN & VEGAN
BURGERS—PLUS
TOPPINGS, SIDES,
BUNS, & MORE

THE EXPERIMENT

LUKAS VOLGER

VEGGIE BURGERS EVERY WHICH WAY

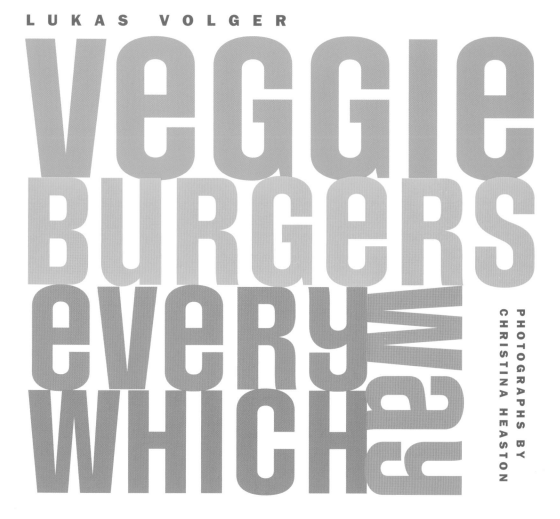

PHOTOGRAPHS BY CHRISTINA HEASTON

Veggie Burgers Every Which Way: *Fresh, Flavorful and Healthy Vegetarian and Vegan Burgers—Plus Toppings, Sides, Buns, and More*

The Experiment, LLC

260 Fifth Avenue

New York, NY 10001-6425

www.theexperimentpublishing.com

Library of Congress Control Number: 2009940036

ISBN 978-1-61519-019-5

Cover design by Susi Oberhelman

Cover photographs and author photograph by Christina Heaston

Text design by Pauline Neuwirth, Neuwirth & Associates, Inc.

Manufactured in China

First printing June 2010

10 9 8 7 6 5 4 3 2 1

In memory of my mom, Pam Volger

INTRODUCTION xv

Veggie Burgers—Why Bother
When It's So Easy to Buy Them in Boxes?

❶ VEGGIE BURGER BASICS 1

INGREDIENTS 2

Beans 2

Rice 7

Bread Crumbs 9

Adapting for Wheat- and Gluten-Free Burgers 10

Egg Substitutes 11

COOKING EQUIPMENT 13

MAKING BURGERS 15

LEFTOVERS 17

❷ BEAN, GRAIN, AND NUT BURGERS 19

Easy Bean Burgers 23

Armenian Lentil Burgers 24

Seeded Edamame Burgers with Brown Rice
and Apples   28

Tuscan White Bean Burgers 32

Baked Falafel Burgers   35

Cashew-Leek Burgers with Bulgur and Lentils   39

Fava Bean Burgers   42

Quinoa, Red Bean, and Walnut Burgers 🄥🄖🄕   45

Red Lentil and Celery Root Burgers 🄥   46

Baked Quinoa Burgers   49

Pub Grub Veggie Burgers   51

③ VEGETABLE BURGERS   53

Best Portobello Burgers 🄥🄖🄕   57

Beet and Brown Rice Burgers 🄥🄖🄕   59

Thai Carrot Burgers   61

Mushroom Burgers with Barley 🄥🄖🄕   64

Beet "Tartare" 🄖🄕   65

Tortilla-Crusted Stuffed Portobello Burgers 🄖🄕   69

Baked Cauliflower Burgers   71

Butternut Squash, Black Bean, and Chestnut Burgers 🄥   74

Spinach-Chickpea Burgers 🄖🄕   77

Sweet Potato Burgers with Lentils and Kale   79

Corn Burgers with Sun-Dried Tomatoes and Goat Cheese   83

Curried Eggplant and Tomato Burgers 🄖🄕🄥   85

④ TOFU, SEITAN, AND TVP BURGERS   87

Chipotle Black Bean Burgers 🄥   91

WaterCourse Foods Tempeh Burgers 🄥🄖🄕   92

Tofu and Chard Burgers Ⓥ 95

Seitan Burgers with Mango BBQ Sauce Ⓥ 97

Smoked Tofu Burgers Ⓥ 101

"Garden" Burgers 103

Ginger-Soy Tempeh Burgers ⓋⒼⒻ 105

⑤ BURGER BUNS 107

Basic Burger Buns 111

Whole-Wheat Burger Buns 115

Corn Bread Buns 117

Pretzel Rolls 119

Gluten-Free Burger Bread 122

⑥ SIDES: SALADS AND FRIES 123

Watermelon and Citrus Salad ⓋⒼⒻ 125

Red Cabbage Slaw ⒼⒻ 127

Roasted Corn Salad ⓋⒼⒻ 128

Raw Kale Salad with Apples and Candied Walnuts ⓋⒼⒻ 130

Beet, Pickle, and Apple Salad ⓋⒼⒻ 132

Black Olive and Roasted Potato Salad with Arugula ⓋⒼⒻ 135

Barley Salad with Beets and Goat Cheese 136

Classic Baked Fries ⓋⒼⒻ 139

Cumin-Spiked Roasted Sweet Potato Fries ⓋⒼⒻ 142

Rutabaga Fries ⓋⒼⒻ 145

7 CONDIMENTS AND TOPPINGS 147

Quick Pickles **V GF** 151

Frizzled Shallots **V GF** 152

Quick-Pickled Red Onions **V GF** 155

Curried Tomato Relish **V GF** 156

Pomegranate-Sesame Sauce **V GF** 157

Sweet Sesame Glaze **V GF** 158

Mango BBQ Sauce **V GF** 159

Four Simple Yogurt Sauces **GF** 161

Cucumber-Yogurt Sauce 161

Curried Yogurt Sauce 162

Tahini-Yogurt Sauce 162

Almond-Yogurt Sauce 162

Acknowledgments 165
Resources 167
Index 169
About the Author 174

V = vegan   **GF** = gluten-free

veggie BURGERS
EVERY WHICH WAY

VEGGIE BURGERS—
WHY BOTHER WHEN IT'S SO
EASY TO BUY THEM IN BOXES?

A VEGGIE BURGER is no mere approximation of a hamburger. Aside from their shared circular shapes, the two have very little in common. So why is it that veggie burgers are so often used as boring stand-ins for hamburgers? And why do we call them "burgers" in the first place? It seems that veggie burgers have been unfairly represented, and it's about time to champion them as their own independent category of food.

Over the past few decades, packaged and frozen veggie burgers have developed a loyal following among vegetarians and vegans, and I'm frequently baffled as to how this happened. I'm a long-time veggie burger enthusiast, but I've never been a fan of those. I don't like the rubbery texture, and I don't like all the salt and the often-cryptic ingredients—can someone tell me what modified vegetable gum is, or autolyzed yeast extract? Can I buy either of them at the grocery store? Most of all, I don't like that processed flavor, present even in the ones that claim to be made only from identifiable ingredients; I find it to be suggestive of fast-food joints and stinky microwaves. It seems that most people settle for these as a quick fix: as a snack, an easy dinner, or something to pop in the microwave on your lunch break. When I talked to vegetarians and vegans as I was working on this book, even accomplished cooks admitted that it had never occurred to them to make veggie burgers themselves—despite eating them for years. Many, however, told me of their favorite store-bought brands and the restaurants that serve the best renditions. Now, I've long known that veggie burgers have a central role in the diets of vegetarians and vegans (and many omnivores as well), but I didn't realize how limited our collective curiosity appears to be when it comes to this particular staple.

Since 1982, when Gregory Sams, a British nutritionist and entrepreneur, christened the original "VegeBurger," which was a dry mix packet, we've opened up to different styles of eating. These new styles have appeared in response to the industrialization of modern food: Many of us want to know exactly what is in the food we eat, where it originates, how it's been prepared, and what its environmental and ethical toll is. At the same time, hamburgers continue to reign as our easiest calories, a mentality that likely reflects a culture that has grown accustomed to easy-access, high-calorie, fast food. After all, you can get a hamburger without having to park your car. And in the tradition of the classic barbecue or cookout, just throw a few burgers and hot dogs on the grill, grab a tub of potato salad, a watermelon, some beer and soda, and eat to your heart's content. This is where, I think, veggie burgers asserted themselves: as a peace offering. *Here*, someone might have said, flopping what looked like a frozen hockey puck on the grill, *we wouldn't want you to feel left out*. Because when we think of veggie burgers, these are often the terms, even for those of us who've been eating them for practically our entire lives. We don't eat them because we like them, per se; we eat them because it's the only way we can take part in the culinary custom. Veggie burgers have been treated as an afterthought to a meat-fest, and we've accepted them as some kind of consolation prize.

These frozen burgers, if not served as a "special request" alongside a spread of meats, appear rather insultingly designed to be consumed by just one person. How else to explain the individual wrappers, akin to frozen TV dinners or individually packaged, frozen burritos? It sends the message that a veggie burger isn't something that any number of people would all want to eat at the same time, that one would never be inclined to serve a veggie burger at a dinner party, or, worse yet: *You wouldn't want to eat* that *in public!*

No more, I say! A hearty, delicious, easy, homemade veggie burger is within your reach! And there's more good news: I have collected here over thirty of them to choose from. And your friends will want to eat them too—even the ones who eat meat.

From the beginning of my interest in veggie burgers my approach has been to regard the veggie burger as a cuisine unto itself: It is far more varied than its meat-based counterpart and ungoverned by any particular geographic cuisine or generally accepted set of rules. The veggie burger is a very accepting category of food. Which brings up the question: What *is* a veggie burger, then, besides some-

thing that is meatless and shaped like a disc? I'll show rather than tell by sharing a few examples: Curried Eggplant and Tomato Burgers (page 85), Baked Quinoa Burgers (page 49), Spinach-Chickpea Burgers (page 77), Armenian Lentil Burgers (page 24), Thai Carrot Burgers (page 61), Beet and Brown Rice Burgers (page 59). What these burgers have in common is that they are all unique expressions of the colors, textures, and tastes of the assorted fresh ingredients from which they are prepared—and that they started out as seeds in the ground.

Use the freshest vegetables and ingredients you can get your hands on, whether purchased at the farmers' market, delivered in your weekly CSA box, grown in your backyard, picked up at a produce stand along the highway, or selected from the produce aisle of your grocery store. Your veggie burgers will only be as good as the ingredients that go into them. As I'll explain briefly in the next chapter, I prefer to use organic "whole foods" as frequently as possible: ingredients that have been fussed with the least before they come into my possession (minimally processed, unrefined). You won't find any Italian dressing mixes or cans of cream of mushroom soup showing up as a secret ingredient in my recipes.

I've been eating veggie burgers since I was a teenager, and thinking consciously about them for almost as long. *Veggie Burgers Every Which Way* assembles literally every veggie burger I can think of—as well as a few that other cooks have dreamt up. You might be surprised by some of the unconventional burgers found here. Try the gluten-free Beet "Tartare" (page 65), or Fava Bean Burgers (page 42), or the delicious vegan Tofu and Chard Burgers (page 95) for some surprising spins. Or if you want to keep things more conventional, I suggest the vegan Chipotle Black Bean Burgers (page 91), the "Garden" Burgers (page 103; the closest approximation of a store-bought burger that I've concocted), or the Pub-Grub Veggie Burgers (page 51). While you're making your own veggie burgers, I encourage you to try your hand at making your own burger buns as well; included here are both vegan recipes and a gluten-free one. There are also some delicious, healthy takes on the traditional burger sides. I could (and often do) prepare all of these recipes frequently, but the Rutabaga Fries (page 145) have become a particular favorite—and if you've not often cooked with rutabagas (who has?), they may be a revelation. In the end, I hope—and am willing to bet—you'll no longer have the impulse to reach for the frozen package.

veggie BURGER Basics

In many ways, veggie burgers are a simple endeavor: take beans, grains, tofu, a vegetable—or a combination thereof—and using binders and starches and complementary flavors, make the mixture malleable and form it into patties. The trick is to get the balance right. Too many bread crumbs, for example, will wash out the flavor; too few and you run the risk of the burger squeezing out the other end of the bun when you bite into it. The recipes in this book will produce a flavorful burger that will hold its shape: In this chapter I'll expand on a few of the principles behind the recipes.

INGREDIENTS

▶ BEANS

Beans are an essential ingredient in many of these recipes. There are hundreds of types of beans on the market, especially with the ever-growing popularity of heirloom beans. I'm willing to bet that all of them would be good in a veggie burger, and I encourage you to seek them out and try cooking with them. On pages 19 and 20, I go into greater detail about the types of beans used in this book and their various merits in veggie burger recipes.

Canned beans are on many occasions a necessary shortcut—since using canned beans is, by leaps and bounds, less time-consuming than cooking your own. However, I urge you to at least have the *intention* of cooking your own beans every now and then.

Cooking with dried beans does take some time. Most beans benefit from having a day to soak, and then some beans can take up to a few hours to cook. But the time beans require isn't active time—

most of the cooking and soaking doesn't even require your supervision. And what can I say to make you believe me when I say the flavor of dried beans cooked at home is far superior to the flavor of canned beans—even the best canned beans? You might be surprised to find that properly home-cooked beans are supple and tender and hold their shape, unlike the filmy mush that so often comes out of a can; they have a clean, distinctive flvor that is neither salty nor cloying.

If you are going to use canned beans, I urge you to spend the extra 60 cents or so on an organic, sodium-free, better-quality brand. In my experience, organic is better than not organic. As the organic farming and food-production companies become even more industrialized, one certainly can't just accept this as a fail-safe rule. (And, as is sometimes worth pointing out when movements become faddish, organic does not always mean healthier!) But I do find that organic foods taste better, and I rest easier knowing that they haven't been doused in chemicals and fertilizers.

Whatever the canned beans you use, be sure to rinse them thoroughly: cover with water in a large bowl and rub the beans gently with your fingers so as to thoroughly clean them of the liquid they were canned in; pour off the water and rinse again.

A NOTE ABOUT CANNED BEANS: One 14-ounce can of beans yields roughly 1½ cups beans.

COOKING Beans

BEGIN BY RINSING dried beans in plenty of cold water and picking through them for small rocks, immature or overdry beans, and other debris. Most beans (except for small beans like lentils and split peas) require soaking before they can be cooked. In my experience, soaking the beans will not only lessen the cooking time by allowing them to begin to reconstitute before being put over heat, but the final texture is far better than when the beans have not been soaked.

By rinsing, soaking, and refreshing the water you are also removing some of the sugars that cause gas. There is some contention on this matter. Some cooks argue that changing the soaking and cooking water does prevent gas, while others argue that the soaking and rinsing and repeating is an entirely unnecessary and ineffective step. Others advocate adding a sprig of epazote (a leafy herb native to Central America and used frequently in Mexican cuisine) to the beans while they are cooking. My feeling is that everyone reacts to beans differently, and in my experience presoaked and thoroughly rinsed beans do not cause any alarming gas. But frankly, I think folks need to just relax on this issue.

There are two soaking methods:

OVERNIGHT SOAK: In a large bowl, cover the beans by three to four times their volume (the beans will double to triple in volume, and you want to ensure that they do not rise above the water level during the soak); cover and let stand overnight. The next day, drain off the water, rinse the beans, and proceed with cooking.

QUICK(ER) SOAK: Place the beans in the cooking pot with water three to four times their volume. Bring the water to a boil and boil for a couple minutes. Remove from the heat, cover the pot, and let sit for at least 1 hour, or up to 4 hours. When the soak is done, drain off the water, rinse the beans, and proceed with cooking.

TO COOK: Put the soaked beans in a pot covered with water by three or four times their volume. Feel free to add aromatics to the cooking liquid: half an onion, a bay leaf, a few sage leaves, some garlic—but hold off on the salt (see below). Bring to

a boil. Reduce the heat to a gentle simmer, partially cover, and cook the beans until tender. The best way to know when the beans are done—and this is almost universally true for food—is to taste. Cooking times vary greatly. Black beans, chickpeas, white kidney, and cannellini beans all take between 1 and 1½ hours. Small, unsoaked beans like lentils and split peas will take 20 to 40 minutes.

Salting is recommended: Salt the beans—1 teaspoon per cup of dried beans—toward the end of the cooking, during the last 5 to 10 minutes or so; if you salt too early, the skins of the beans will tighten and resist water absorption.

LEFTOVERS: A bowl of warm, freshly cooked beans drizzled with olive oil and a sprinkling of salt and pepper is one of my favorite snacks. Also, I can find uses for almost any leftover beans in salads, soups, and as spreads for sandwiches.

For excess leftover cooked beans, store them covered with water in an airtight container in the refrigerator. They will keep for 3 to 4 days, sometimes up to a week if you change the water every other day. The smell will be the giveaway—if they are going bad they will have an off, "fishy" odor, and they will begin to break apart. Cooked beans, stored in water or their cooking liquid, can be kept in the freezer for months.

VARIATION: In Amanda Hesser's 2001 *New York Times* profile of Paola di Mauro—the mentor of Italian culinary powerhouses like Mario Batali and Lidia Bastianich—she anecdotally mentions an alternate cooking method for beans. You'll have to tend to the beans more actively—it's a bit like making risotto, as you stir in the hot water only as the beans absorb it—but it's a fun alternative and a good way to impress a date.

Pour cold water over the presoaked beans just to cover—*not* three to four times the volume of the beans—and bring to boil. Reduce the heat to a gentle simmer, and then place a large heatproof bowl on top of the pot and fill it with water, so that it functions as a lid or double-boiler. As the beans begin to soak up the water, add a ladleful of the hot water from the simmering bowl on top. The cooking time will be roughly the same as in the usual method.

▶ RICE

Rice is used in many of the recipes here to stretch the base vegetable, bean, or other protein and to give the burgers body and texture. Many types of rice are delicious, but because of the nutritional benefits of brown rice, I use it almost exclusively in veggie burgers. I usually opt for a long-grain brown rice—brown basmati is my favorite—because it has a delicious, buttery flavor and holds its shape well. White rice can be substituted—in fact, almost any rice works well in a veggie burger. Using leftover takeout rice is also an excellent idea. But as it's economical and not difficult to make your own, here are instructions for cooking it yourself. Admittedly, there are as many methods for cooking rice as there are cooks, so my method should by no means be taken as the final word.

* * *

COOKING RICE

GENERALLY, RICE WILL double in size when cooked.

On the issue of whether or not rice should be rinsed and presoaked, cooks seem to be split down the middle. It used to be that rice needed to be cleaned prior to cooking, but nowadays it's argued that this step is unnecessary and can be achieved by just picking through the dry rice for debris. Furthermore, rinsing the rice rids it of some of its starch. This can be a good thing if you want rice that does not stick together. But if you prefer sticky rice, omit the rinsing.

Brown basmati rice, my favorite, benefits from a few rinses (I prefer the texture after the starch has been washed off). Begin by washing the rice thoroughly: Place it a large bowl, cover with cold water, and then rub the grains with your hands. Drain off excess water. Rinse the rice three or four times, until the water is no longer murky.

Many cooks advocate presoaking long-grain rices like basmati, arguing that this protects its delicate flavor and improves the structure by giving the rice a chance to absorb some liquid before applying heat.

To soak, cover the rice by about 2 inches of water and let stand for at least 30 minutes, or up to a few hours. Carefully pour or strain off as much of the soaking water as possible without losing the grains.

For cooking, the ratio of presoaked brown rice to water is 1:1½. I find that after soaking, less water is needed, so if you omit the soak, I recommend a ratio of 1:2. (But again, every cook has his or her own method: For unsoaked rice, renowned vegetarian cookbook author Deborah Madison says 1:2½ while vegetarian world cuisine matriarch Madhur Jaffrey says 1:2.)

Combine water and rice in a heavy-bottomed saucepan into which the rice fits snugly and place over medium heat. When the water begins to boil, turn the heat down as low as possible and cover the pot with a tight-fitting lid. It's important that the steam doesn't escape during cooking. If the lid doesn't fit tightly, seal the pot first with a piece of aluminum foil and then place the lid on top of it. Let cook for 30 minutes (25 minutes if using white rice). After 30 minutes, remove from the heat and let stand for at least 10 minutes.

VARIATION: BOILED RICE

With so much fretting over how much water is needed in order to correctly steam rice, it can be a relief to just boil it. The only disadvantage is that many of the nutrients are poured off with the cooking water. Boiling is not recommended for any rice where you want to preserve the starchiness, like Arborio, which is used in risotto.

Bring a pot of salted water to boil (you need not measure the water as long as it generously exceeds the volume of the rice). Add rice and cook for 10 to 15 minutes, until tender. Drain and proceed with the recipe.

✳ ✳ ✳

► BREAD CRUMBS

In nonvegetarian cooking, bread crumbs make meats malleable. They prevent things like meatballs and crab cakes from becoming too dense by aerating the protein and soaking up additional moisture. The same is true of veggie burgers. While no one wants a veggie burger that is mostly bread, the starch is a necessary element. Unseasoned, store-bought bread crumbs are fine to use.

But you can save money and have more control by making your own. Whenever I have bread that begins to go stale, I rip it up into small pieces and put it in a bag in the freezer. I don't bother to trim the crusts off and am completely impartial when it comes to what goes into the bag—pita bread, rolls, buns, white bread, baguette, whole-wheat bread, etc. When the bag is full, I make bread crumbs.

Making and Toasting Bread Crumbs

Four standard slices of bread yield about a cup of bread crumbs.

Preheat the oven to 325°F.

Tear the bread into roughly ½-inch pieces and pulse in a food processor until ground. Transfer to a baking sheet and toast in the oven for 15 to 20 minutes, until uniformly golden and crisp. Carefully stir the crumbs every 5 minutes, more frequently if your oven has uneven heat. Toasted crumbs can be kept for weeks in an airtight container.

Some bread crumb recipes recommend tossing or quickly sautéing toasted bread crumbs in olive oil. This can be done when the crumbs are used as a topping, either in baked dishes like casseroles or sprinkled over cooked vegetables. For veggie burgers, it's an unnecessary step.

NOTE: If you don't have a food processor, tear the bread into pieces as small as possible and then toast in the oven. When cool, place the toasted crumbs in a sturdy, airtight bag, and place the bag flat between a sandwich of kitchen towels. Grind them into crumbs up by going over them with a rolling pin, flipping the bag and shaking it periodically.

Additionally, some recipes here call for *panko,* Japanese bread crumbs that are crisp and white and larger than typical store-bought bread crumbs. They can now be found at most supermarkets; if not, Asian markets will have several different brands to choose from.

▶ ADAPTING FOR WHEAT- AND GLUTEN-FREE BURGERS

Gluten-free **GF** bread crumbs sold at grocery stores are often not much more than rice flour or corn meal, and thus lack the absorption properties of wheat-based bread. I wasn't impressed with the results I had when using these store-bought GF bread crumbs. I found that grinding and toasting crumbs from store-bought gluten-free breads produced much better results (just follow the instructions above). Homemade gluten-free bread crumbs can be substituted in any of the recipes here that call for bread crumbs.

But I've included many recipes here that are gluten-free by their own volition. As anyone who adheres to a gluten-free diet knows, there are many, many alternate "flours" out there that are made from beans, nuts, and grains. My favorite gluten-free recipes feature flours made from chickpeas or brown rice.

Flours—particularly specialty flours and gluten-free flour blends—can have significantly longer shelf lives if they are stored in the refrigerator or freezer. Transfer the flour to an airtight container and refrigerate or freeze and they will keep for months. I find that mason jars work well for this purpose. If you can find a store that sells dry goods in bulk, you'll save yourself space and money purchasing only what you need.

> **TIP: Alternate flours are often expensive, especially given that many recipes require only small amounts. With any bean or grain flour, you can easily make your own. Grind small portions of uncooked whole beans or grains in a clean, dry spice grinder or blender and sift out the large chunks.**

A NOTE ABOUT WHEAT- AND GLUTEN-FREE: If you adhere to a gluten-free diet, you are probably highly adept at reading food labels. I've made efforts to mark which items need their gluten-free counterparts, but please use your own experience, instincts, and knowledge when shopping for ingredients.

If you're new to gluten- and wheat-free eating, here is a brief summary: People who are on a GF diet are split into two camps. First, there are those who have been diagnosed with celiac disease, a genetically determined disease where any gluten consumed injures the lining of the small intestine and makes digestion difficult and painful. The second camp is of people who have an allergy to wheat. While digestion-related symptoms are also prevalent in people with wheat allergies, other allergic reactions are triggered, like skin rashes, inflammation, headaches, and nausea. These reactions can range from minor to life-threatening, similar to how people respond to nut allergies.

In addition to traditional breads, baked goods, and pasta, many other foods contain gluten. Generally, one must avoid all wheat—white flour, whole-wheat flour, barley, rye, oats, spelt—and wheat by-products. Malt is a derivative of gluten and thus cannot be consumed; it shows up in several aged vinegars and drinks. Foods as wide-ranging as beer, soy sauce, imitation vanilla extract (as well as most other imitation extracts), ketchup, and baking powder can contain gluten. (Most of these items have gluten-free counterparts, which are usually clearly marked as such.) Whenever the words "stabilizer," "starch," and "emulsifier" show up on package labels, it is often a red flag for wheat gluten. Many, many foods *are* naturally gluten-free, however. Rice, nuts, beans, fruits, vegetables, and dairy are all naturally gluten-free. Eliminating gluten can be an invitation to broaden one's culinary horizons by cooking with grains that are traditionally overlooked, like quinoa, millet, and amaranth.

If you're trying out a wheat-free diet for the first time, there is a wealth of information online about what foods to avoid and what types of foods can be substituted for them.

▶ EGG SUBSTITUTES

About half of the recipes included here are egg- and dairy-free. Without eggs, some other kind of binder is needed to help hold the burgers together and give them rise. The following is an incomplete list of ingredients that deliver these properties:

STEAMED POTATO AND POTATO STARCH: In veggie burgers, the combination of steamed potato and potato starch is one of my favorite egg substitutes because it contributes a pleasant flavor. But use caution: Steamed potato works as a binder but does not expand as it cooks as eggs do; if overused, potato can make the burgers dense. The addition of a small amount of potato starch helps to resolve the density problem by limiting the amount of cooked potato but making use of its binding properties.

I prefer to use Yukon Gold potatoes because I like the flavor. To steam, peel the potato, cut it into ½-inch pieces, and place in a steaming basket. Bring a bit of water in a small saucepan to a simmer, add the basket, and cover. Cook for 8 to 10 minutes, until the potato can be effortlessly pierced with a fork or skewer. (Alternatively, roasted or boiled potatoes can be substituted.) Allow to cool slightly, and then mash with a fork. Half a small potato plus 1 teaspoon potato starch is roughly the equivalent of an egg.

Most grocery stores carry potato starch, either in the ethnic food aisle (where it's inexpensive) or along with the specialty flour blends (where it is expensive). In addition, if you can find a store that sells dry goods in bulk, potato starch is usually found there.

VITAL WHEAT GLUTEN: Vital wheat gluten is what's left of flour after all the starch has been rinsed off. Seitan—"vegetarian duck"—is seasoned, cooked vital wheat gluten. In veggie burgers it makes a decent egg substitute, though sometimes the raw flour taste comes through for me. Vital wheat gluten will seize up when you add it to the burger mixture as it binds with the liquids (combining vital wheat gluten with water produces a rubbery dough), so be sure to add it as the last ingredient, sprinkling it evenly over the mixture and quickly working it in with your hands.

GROUND FLAXSEED: For the equivalent of a single egg, take 1 tablespoon flaxseed and grind to powder in a spice grinder. (Alternatively, use 2½ teaspoons ground flaxseed.) Whisk in 3 tablespoons water until it emulsifies. Flax has a distinctive, grainy-grassy flavor, so this isn't going to be the subtlest substitution. But in recipes like Seeded Edamame Burgers with Brown Rice and Apples (page 28), the additional flax flavor adds a terrific dimension.

EGG REPLACER: There are a few brands of "egg replacer" on the market and a few of them are vegetarian only (usually because they contain gelatin or algae); be sure to check the label. Many vegan cooks swear by Ener-G Egg Replacer. I do not expressly call for egg replacer in any of the recipes here, but it is a viable alternative to eggs in the burgers.

COOKING EQUIPMENT

Making veggie burgers is not a difficult culinary endeavor, but there are a few cooking tools that make the job a bit easier. Aside from the standard *batterie de cuisine* (good knives, a big, heavy cutting board, mixing bowls, a spatula, an oven thermometer, etc.), the following items will come in handy:

SIEVE: A sieve makes the job of cleaning beans, rice, and grains infinitely easier, especially if you can find one that fits inside a larger bowl so that the contents of the strainer can be submerged in water and then lifted out. Plastic colanders have holes that are too large for small grains and beans.

SALAD SPINNER: A salad spinner makes the job of cleaning greens and leafy herbs—such as spinach, kale, chard, parsley, and cilantro—a snap. The ideal salad spinner is essentially just a colander that fits inside a larger plastic bowl and has some kind of spinning mechanism that rids the greens of water. If you choose one that does not drain water out the bottom, the bowl that the colander fits into will come in handy for submerging greens and swishing them around to clean off dirt.

FOOD PROCESSOR Here's the bad news: For many of the burgers in this book, there isn't really a way around using a food processor. A food processor will blitz everything up with minimal effort. They come in many sizes, ranging from mini-choppers to industrial-size Robot Coupes. A miniature food processor can be used for veggie burgers as long as you process in small batches. A blender is unfortunately an insufficient substitute because it requires too much liquid in order to get the mixture moving (you'd end up with a veggie burger smoothie). But I lived for many years without a food processor, so I understand your predicament if you don't own one. Not all the recipes here require a food processor, and where applicable, I've listed alternate preparation methods.

POTATO MASHER: This comes in handy for mashing beans and vegetables when a fork doesn't seem to be enough for the job. I prefer a "wire" potato masher to the kind that is a flat piece of metal with diamond-shaped holes.

MEAT GRINDER: Seriously! Well, I made veggie burgers with a friend who has a meat grinder attachment on her KitchenAid stand mixer, and it did a beautiful job of blitzing the vegetable-and-bean mixtures. By all means, don't go buy a meat grinder (much less a KitchenAid) just for this purpose. But if you have one lying around, you might discover some surprising uses for it with these recipes.

CAST-IRON SKILLET: Cast-iron skillets are great because they are significantly less expensive than other oven-safe skillets, they heat evenly, and they improve with use, developing their own unique patina by absorbing the oils of what cooks in them. (I started developing many of the recipes in this book using a new 10-inch cast-iron skillet, and I now have a wonderfully seasoned pan.) Cast-iron skillets come in many different sizes—anywhere from 6 to 18 inches in diameter. In addition to my 10-inch skillet, I have a small 6-inch one, which is perfect for cooking a single veggie burger. But in general I get the most use out of the 10-inch skillet. Just be sure to care for your cast-iron skillet correctly: no harsh soaps, no submerging in soapy water, no scraping clean with steel wool or other abrasive sponges. To clean, just quickly and gently wipe out the pan using warm water and a small amount of dish soap, and then blot dry with a clean towel (if left to air dry, your skillet will begin to rust).

NONSTICK, OVEN-SAFE SAUTÉ PAN: Ideally all of your skillets and sauté pans are oven-safe, but if you're striving to cook with less oil (I don't worry much about that here because most of these recipes are very low in fat), then the nonstick pan is the way to go. It will be a bit of an investment, but a good one.

FRYDADDY: If you've any plans to deep-fry with any regularity, a FryDaddy—literally a metal bucket that plugs into an electrical socket and keeps oil at the proper 375°F for frying—makes the job infinitely easier and cleaner. The fact that it maintains the temperature for you—no more finessing with the burner to get the oil to stay at the right temperature—is reason enough to own one. There are a few burgers here that lend themselves to deep-frying, but it's the French fries that will make the FryDaddy earn its keep.

MAKING BURGERS

▶ SHAPING BURGERS

I prefer my veggie burgers to be moderate in size: about 4 inches in diameter and ¾ inch thick. If you shape the burgers any larger, you run the risk of having them fall apart when you flip them. If they're any smaller, they'll seem like an afterthought to the hamburger bun.

Veggie burger "sliders" are also a fun variation. Simply shape rounded tablespoons of the mixture into small patties and then

sauté. See note below regarding cooking time and cooking method.

▶ COOKING METHODS

I've been cooking veggie burgers for a long time—for years before I began to work on this book. And I cooked them in many different ways over the years: in a sauté pan, in the oven, on the barbecue, and [gulp] occasionally in the microwave. As I began to develop the recipes that appear in this book, I experimented with *many* different ways of cooking veggie burgers. Based on all of my past experience and then my more recent experimenting, I've settled on what I believe to be the one almost universally fail-safe method:

■ **BEST VEGGIE BURGER COOKING METHOD: Preheat the oven to 375°F. In an oven-safe skillet or nonstick sauté pan, heat oil over medium-high heat. When hot, add the burgers and brown, turning once, for 6 to 10 minutes total. Transfer the pan to the oven and bake for 12 to 15 minutes, until the burgers are firm and cooked through. If cooking a larger quantity than will fit in your skillet,** brown the burgers in batches and then transfer them to a baking sheet or roasting pan before going into the oven.

This combination of first "searing" the burgers and then finishing in the oven is the same method that restaurants use on cuts of meat. I realize it's a fairly nontraditional approach to veggie burgers. I repeatedly found that when the size of burgers I wanted to cook were cooked only in a sauté pan, they weren't fully cooked in the center, forcing me to either overcook the exterior or add more bread crumbs than I'd like so as to dry out the mixture. Just baking the burgers is fine, but in my opinion the absence of a crisp, "charred" exterior is far too much of a compromise. My method resolves this issue and offers the best of both worlds: a crispy exterior and fully cooked interior. It also facilitates a slightly wetter mixture—which means that fewer bread crumbs are needed—because the burgers will dry out a bit and firm up in the oven. Most of the recipes included here use this method, but if you're not persuaded by my advocacy of the method and prefer alternate methods, I offer the guidelines below:

■ TO PANFRY: **In a skillet, heat oil over medium-high heat. When hot, add the burgers. Let sizzle for about a minute and then turn the heat to medium-low. Cook for 5 to 7 minutes, until browned, and then flip and finish cooking on the other side. You may want to cover the pan for 2 or 3 minutes of the cooking time so as to cook the burgers through. But be judicious about doing this, as you may inadvertently steam the burgers.**

■ TO BAKE: **This is a good method for burgers that are too delicate for the frying pan, such as Baked Cauliflower Burgers (page 71) and Baked Falafel Burgers (page 35). Preheat the oven to 375°F. Lightly grease a baking sheet, roasting pan, or other oven-safe pan. Bake the burgers for 20 to 25 minutes, flipping halfway through, until firmed and lightly browned on each side.**

■ TO GRILL: **Just about everyone— even vegans and vegetarians— likes food that's been prepared on an outdoor grill or barbecue. When** you use a grill to cook veggie burgers, you can get decent results by treating it as more of an oven than a grill. Cook the burgers on either a small baking sheet or a double layer of heavy-duty aluminum foil. The burgers will require about 15 minutes of cooking time over medium-high heat. Flip them halfway through. The strength of any grill's heat varies greatly, so be sure to keep an eye on the burgers. Watch for them to brown on the exterior and firm up, indicating that they are fully cooked through.

- **COOKING "SLIDERS": Sauté the sliders in oil, turning once, for 6 to 10 minutes total. It is not necessary to transfer them to the oven to finish heating. To keep a batch of sliders warm, place on a parchment-lined baking sheet in a 275°F oven.**

A NOTE ON OIL: Unless otherwise specified in these recipes, I recommend using an oil that is mild, is as minimally processed as possible, and that has a high smoking point. I call for olive oil throughout the book, but feel free to substitute another oil, like grapeseed or canola oil, that you prefer.

LEFTOVERS

Most of the burgers, uncooked or cooked, will keep for 3 to 5 days in the refrigerator. Uncooked burgers will keep for up to 2 months in the freezer. A whiff is usually enough to determine if they're still good to eat, but especially if they've been in the refrigerator a few days (and perhaps not stored under optimal conditions—see below), you may want to taste a little bit of a refrigerated burger before proceeding to eat it.

Keep **UNCOOKED** patties in an airtight container, layered between parchment or wax paper, or sealed up with plastic wrap on a plate. Remove from the refrigerator an hour before you want to cook them, as they will be more difficult to cook through if they are still cold. Then continue with your cooking method of choice. Uncooked veggie burgers that don't contain tofu, tempeh, or seitan will freeze relatively well, but they will have become significantly wetter when they thaw. Before cooking, be sure to allow the burgers to thaw completely (leave them in the refrigerator overnight) and blot them dry with paper towels. If the mixture still seems too wet, fold in a few teaspoons of bread crumbs and reshape the patty. To freeze, wrap the burgers individually in plastic wrap and place in an airtight container or resealable plastic bag.

Leftover **COOKED** burgers can be reheated in a 300°F oven on a lightly greased baking sheet for about 15 minutes, or in the microwave for 2 minutes on high. I also enjoy eating them cold or at room temperature as a filling for a sandwich. I don't recommend freezing cooked veggie burgers, as the additional moisture that comes with freezing them makes the texture mushy.

2

Bean, Grain, and Nut Burgers

Beans are arguably the ultimate veggie burger ingredient. They're a good source of protein (as well as fiber and other nutrients) for vegetarians and vegans, are inexpensive, will keep for months in your cupboards with minimal fuss, and—most importantly—are an expansive culinary foundation. They play a crucial role in many of the veggie burgers in this book, giving them their primary flavor and enhancing their overall structure.

The following are the beans most used in this cookbook:

* **BLACK BEANS, ALSO KNOWN AS TURTLE BEANS:** Black beans have shiny black skins and a velvety interior and are naturally

high in fiber. They are a staple of Latin cuisine and are famously good in veggie burgers.

* CHICKPEAS, ALSO KNOWN AS GARBANZO BEANS: The foundation for hummus, chickpeas are higher in protein than many other beans and have an unmistakable "eggy" taste. They're a dominant aspect of Indian and Mediterranean cuisines.

* EDAMAME: Edamame are simply young soybeans that were frozen rather than dried. They cook in about 3 minutes and their tender, vegetal flavor and bright green color are entirely preserved. Dried soybeans take eons to cook—3 hours or more—such that it oftentimes seems like a better use of your time and energy to just grow the beans yourself.

* KIDNEY BEANS: Red kidney beans have a mild flavor and are large and starchy and thus make an excellent binder in place of eggs for vegan veggie burgers. White kidney beans are similar in texture and flavor and can be used interchangeably with navy, cannellini, and Great Northern beans (see below).

* LENTILS: There are over fifty different types of lentils available worldwide and they come in a rainbow of colors, but the three most commonly available are brown, red, and green lentils. My favorite is the dark green French lentil because it has a slightly more defined, earthy flavor and holds its shape after cooking. Brown and red lentils are most often split and thus have shorter cooking times. They will disintegrate after cooking—which in some veggie burger recipes is exactly what you want.

* NAVY, CANNELLINI, AND GREAT NORTHERN BEANS: These three are often grouped together. Cannellini are the largest and Great Northerns are the smallest, but otherwise the three are very similar, with white skins and creamy interiors. Cannellini arguably have the creamiest interior, but I find that as far as veggie burgers go, they are interchangeable.

For cooking times and guidelines, see page 4.

EASY BEAN BURGER

Easy Bean Burgers

THESE SIMPLE BURGERS can be made from almost any medium or large bean. My favorites are chickpeas, black beans, and red beans, but I find that this recipe is also a good place to experiment with heirloom beans, such as red calypso beans or moon beans. (You can also use any of the hundreds of different beans available at farmers' markets and through the internet—just be sure to choose medium to large starchy beans.) Feel free to use a combination of beans. And if ever called upon to cook for a crowd in a pinch, multiply this recipe by three, and use three full cans of different beans.

▶ MAKES FOUR 4-INCH BURGERS

1 ½ cups cooked beans

2 eggs, beaten

½ cup roughly chopped fresh parsley

¼ cup grated Parmesan

2 teaspoons Dijon mustard

½ teaspoon salt

¼ teaspoon freshly ground black pepper

Squeeze of fresh lemon juice

¾ cup toasted bread crumbs, plus more if needed

2 tablespoons olive oil

1. Preheat the oven to 375°F.
2. In a mixing bowl, mash the beans using a potato masher or fork. Fold in the eggs, parsley, Parmesan, mustard, salt, pepper, and lemon juice. Fold in the bread crumbs, adding more if the mixture is too loose. Let sit for 5 to 10 minutes for the crumbs to soak up some moisture. Adjust seasonings. Shape into 4 patties.
3. In an oven-safe skillet or nonstick sauté pan, heat the oil over medium-high heat. When hot, add the patties and cook until browned on each side, 6 to 10 minutes total. Transfer the pan to the oven and bake for 12 to 15 minutes, until the burgers are firm and cooked through.

▶ PREP AND COOK TIME: 30 minutes

ARMENIAN LENTIL BURGERS

THE INSPIRATION FOR this burger came from Ani Chamichian, a friend whose family hails from Armenia. The warm spices—doubly enforced by using whole spices as aromatics with the lentils, and then added again to the veggie burger mixture—beautifully complement the earthy lentils. It's particularly good with Cucumber-Yogurt Sauce (page 161).

► MAKES FOUR 4-INCH BURGERS

LENTILS

1 cup French (green) lentils

½ onion, cut into two quarters through the stem

2 whole cloves

1 teaspoon olive oil

1-inch piece ginger, cut into two pieces

2 garlic cloves, crushed and peeled

1 cinnamon stick

1 bay leaf

BURGERS

4 tablespoons plus 1 teaspoon olive oil, divided

1 onion, chopped

1¾ teaspoons ground allspice

½ teaspoon ground cinnamon

¼ teaspoon ground cloves

Pinch of cayenne pepper

3 garlic cloves, minced

2 teaspoons grated fresh ginger

2 eggs

¾ cup toasted bread crumbs

⅓ cup roughly chopped fresh parsley

½ teaspoon salt

Squeeze of fresh lemon juice

1. COOK THE LENTILS: Pick through the lentils and rinse thoroughly. Stud each onion quarter with a clove. In a medium saucepan, heat 1 teaspoon oil over medium heat. Add the onion quarters, ginger pieces, crushed garlic, cinnamon stick, and bay leaf. Stir, then cover and cook for 1 minute, until fragrant. Add the lentils and 2 cups water and bring to a boil. Reduce the heat, cover, and simmer for 15 to 20 minutes, until the lentils

ARMENIAN LENTIL BURGER

are tender. Discard the aromatics (the onion, ginger, garlic, cinnamon stick, and bay leaf) and pour off any excess liquid.

2. **PREPARE THE BURGERS:** Preheat the oven to 375°F.

3. Heat 2 tablespoons of the oil over medium-low heat. Add the chopped onion, allspice, ground cinnamon, ground cloves, and cayenne. Cook, stirring frequently, until the onion begins to caramelize, about 12 minutes. Reduce the heat and add the minced garlic and grated ginger. Cook until the onion is fully cooked, about 5 minutes longer.

4. Set aside ½ cup of the cooked lentils. In a food processor, combine the lentils and the onion mixture with the eggs and pulse until thoroughly combined. Transfer to a mixing bowl. Add the reserved lentils, bread crumbs, parsley, salt, and lemon juice. Adjust seasonings. Shape the mixture into 4 patties.

5. In an oven-safe skillet or nonstick sauté pan, heat the remaining 2 tablespoons oil over medium-high heat. When hot, add the patties and cook until browned on each side, 6 to 10 minutes total. Transfer the pan to the oven and bake for 12 to 15 minutes, until the burgers are firm and cooked through.

▶ **PREP TIME:** 1 hour
▶ **DO AHEAD:** Cook lentils

IF YOU can find a spice shop that sells spices in bulk (as opposed to the packaged jars at the supermarket), the flavor of your burgers (and other dishes) will improve dramatically. The spices will simply be fresher, and you will be able to buy small amounts, thus keeping them fresh in your own kitchen as well. Furthermore, it's best to buy spices whole, toast them in a dry skillet, and then grind them with either a mortar and pestle or electric spice grinder. This applies even to black pepper: Try toasting the peppercorns before you fill your pepper mill. While this might add a few extra steps to your cooking, think of the space you'll save in the spice cabinet, not needing to purchase them both whole and ground. You'll save a little money, too!

Seeded Edamame Burgers with Brown Rice and Apples ⓥ ⒼⒻ

HERE'S A BURGER that may sound strange, given that it's studded with sesame and sunflower seeds and apple and seasoned with soy sauce. But it's unexpectedly delicious. The combination makes these simultaneously sweet, savory, *and* refreshing. It's essential that you give the burgers a good sear on high heat when you first cook them. This searing—as well as the molasses—helps form the crust, which in turn holds the burgers together. I like them topped with pepper jelly and thin slices of cold radishes.

▶ MAKES SIX 4-INCH BURGERS

2 tablespoons hulled raw sunflower seeds

1 tablespoon raw sesame seeds

1 cup frozen shelled edamame

2½ tablespoons ground flaxseed (1 tablespoon whole seeds)

1½ cups cooked brown rice

1 apple, peeled, cored, and finely chopped

2 tablespoons brown (or white) rice flour

1 tablespoon molasses

2 teaspoons soy sauce or tamari (GF)

1 teaspoon toasted sesame oil

A few grinds of black pepper

2 tablespoons olive oil

1. In a dry skillet, toast the sunflower seeds over medium-low heat until lightly browned and fragrant, about 5 minutes, swirling the pan periodically. Transfer to a heatproof plate. In the same pan, toast the sesame seeds until golden brown, no more than 2 minutes, swirling or stirring constantly to avoid overcooking and uneven browning. Transfer to the plate with the sunflower seeds.

2. Meanwhile, cook the edamame according to package directions. Transfer the beans to an ice bath to halt the cooking.

3. Whisk together the ground flax and 3 tablespoons water. Transfer to a food processor and add the toasted seeds and edamame. Pulse 10 to 15 times, just until the mixture is evenly chunky.

4. In a mixing bowl, combine the edamame-seed mixture with the rice, apple, flour, molasses, soy sauce, sesame oil, and black pepper. The mixture should be moist and sticky. Adjust seasonings. Shape into 6 patties, flattening to a ½-inch thickness.

5. In a sauté pan, heat the oil over high heat. When hot, add the patties, in batches if necessary to avoid crowding, cooking for 2 minutes. They should sizzle—this will create a nice crust. Reduce the heat to medium and cook for 2 or 3 minutes more. Carefully flip the burgers and cook until browned and firm, 4 to 5 minutes longer.

▶ PREP AND COOK TIME: 20 minutes
▶ DO AHEAD: Toast seeds, cook edamame

MAKING USE OF
LEFTOVER FRESH HERBS

In an ideal world, I would have an herb garden just outside the kitchen window and could pluck two sage leaves or a single sprig of thyme whenever the culinary inspiration strikes. But until that happens, I'll continue purchasing them from the farmers' market and grocery store, where I inevitably must buy more of any one fresh herb than I need. Here are a few things to do with leftover herbs.

DRYING HERBS

A few years ago I took a cooking class in Paris. When the instructor, Paule, brought out a bunch of fresh thyme, one of my classmates asked, "So, for herbs, what do you recommend? Should we buy fresh ones or dried?" Standing erect, Paule raised her wooden spoon in the air and waved it around: "Zis herbs business, I do not understand. You start with ze herbs fresh, and over time ze herbs become dry. *Non?*" What she meant was that there's no reason not to have ready access to both. Since then, I've been drying most of my leftover fresh herbs.

There are several methods, but here are two that work best for me:

1. Tie up the herbs at the stem with kitchen twine. Pierce a small paper bag a few times with a small knife or skewer. Place the bag over the herbs, holding them upright, and close the bag around the stems, tying it with string or kitchen twine. Hang the bag from the stems in a place where it will be out of the way—the corner of a closet or cupboard works best for me—and let hang for a week or two, until the herbs are fully dried. Crunch up the leaves while still inside the

bag, and then pour out the dried leaves, discarding the stems. Store in a small, airtight container.

2. Remove the fresh herb leaves from their stems and mince. Spread out the leaves between layers of dry paper towels. Let these stand for 5 to 8 days, until fully dried. Store in a small, airtight container.

FREEZING HERBS

Freezing works for herbs that hold their shape as they dry (parsley, thyme, mint, and rosemary, for example) rather than ones that wilt and shrivel up (cilantro and dill). Make sure the herbs are clean and dry, then mince them. Place in a small airtight container and keep in the freezer until ready for use. They don't need to be thawed prior to cooking with them. Frozen herbs will work well in salad dress-

ings and cooked dishes—like veggie burgers!—but less well when they are the headlining ingredient, such as in pesto.

INFUSING OILS WITH HERBS

Fresh herbs make wonderful infused oils for salad dressings, marinades, and drizzles. Any herb and combination of herbs can be used to infuse oil, but some of my favorites are basil oil, rosemary oil, tarragon oil, and parsley-thyme-rosemary oil. To make infused oil, wash a handful of sprigs of your favorite herbs and allow them to completely dry. Place the herbs whole in a glass jar or bottle. Warm 1 cup mild olive oil (or more, if desired) over low heat, then carefully pour over the herbs. Let stand for about a week in a cool, dark place, then strain, discarding the solids. The oil will keep for about 2 months.

TUSCAN WHITE BEAN BURGERS

THIS IS INSPIRED by my favorite Italian crostini: white beans and roasted garlic on toasted bread, drizzled with olive oil. I like to top the burgers with a quick pesto of chopped parsley or arugula, olives, and a squeeze of lemon juice, as pictured. As a tasty alternative, nix the bun entirely and serve the burger on a simple salad of arugula dressed with fresh lemon juice and olive oil.

▶ **MAKES FOUR 4-INCH BURGERS**

1 onion, peeled

4 tablespoons plus ½ teaspoon olive oil

1 head garlic

1½ cups cooked white beans (cannellini or navy beans)

1 egg

3 fresh sage leaves, minced

½ cup sliced pitted Kalamata olives

Squeeze of fresh lemon juice

½ cup toasted bread crumbs, or more if needed

Salt

Freshly ground black pepper

1. Caramelize the onions: Cut the onion in half through the stem and then slice into ⅛-inch-thick half-rings. Heat 2 tablespoons of the olive oil in a heavy-bottomed sauté pan over medium-low heat and add the onion, turning to coat. Cook slowly, stirring occasionally and lowering the heat if the onion begins burn, until caramelized, about 30 minutes. Cool.

2. Meanwhile, roast the garlic. There are many methods, but I prefer this one: Break the head of garlic into cloves and clean off most of the papery skins. Toss the cloves in ½ teaspoon of the oil and spread out on a small baking sheet (a toaster oven works great for this). Roast at 300°F for 25 to 30 minutes, shaking the pan and stirring the cloves around frequently, until the largest clove can be effortlessly pierced with a knife. Cool.

3. Preheat the oven to 375°F.

4. In a food processor, purée ½ cup of the beans with half the roasted garlic, half the caramelized onion, the egg, and half the sage.

5. Chop the remaining onion and roasted garlic coarsely and place in a mixing bowl. Add the remaining beans and coarsely mash with a potato masher. Fold in the puréed bean-egg mixture, remaining sage, the olives, and lemon juice. Fold in the bread crumbs, adding more if necessary—just until the mixture begins to pull from the side of the bowl (it will be a wet mixture). Season with salt and pepper. Adjust seasonings. Shape into 4 patties.

6. In an oven-safe skillet or nonstick sauté pan, heat the remaining 2 tablespoons oil over medium-high heat. When hot, add the patties and cook until browned on each side, 6 to 10 minutes total. Transfer the pan to the oven and bake for 12 to 15 minutes, until slightly firmed and cooked through.

▶ **PREP AND COOK TIME:** 1 hour, including cooling time

▶ **DO AHEAD:** Caramelize onions, roast garlic

TUSCAN WHITE BEAN BURGER

BaHeD FaLaFeL BuRGeRS Ⓥ ⒢

IN THIS FALAFEL method, the chickpeas are soaked overnight but not cooked. (If we were deep-frying the burgers rather than baking them, this would be the traditional falafel method.) Store-bought falafel mixes—many of which are wonderful—use ground, unsoaked dried beans, but I find that the soaking makes for a significantly less dense, more delicate and tender falafel. You'll be amazed at how vibrant the flavors are, how the parsley and lemon shine through. Serve with Cucumber-Yogurt Sauce (page 161), Tahini Yogurt Sauce (page 162), or plain tahini along with a squirt of Sriracha, as a nod to the street food that fed me throughout my college years in Manhattan. Unfortunately, cooked chickpeas will not work in this recipe; there will be too much liquid and the burgers will fall apart as they cook.

▶ MAKES FOUR 4-INCH BURGERS

1 cup dried chickpeas, rinsed thoroughly

1 onion, roughly chopped

2 garlic cloves

½ cup roughly chopped fresh parsley

Zest of 1 lemon

Juice of ½ lemon

1 tablespoon toasted cumin seeds

½ teaspoon baking soda (GF)

¾ teaspoon salt

½ teaspoon freshly ground black pepper

¼ teaspoon cayenne pepper

1 tablespoon chickpea or all-purpose flour, if needed

1. Preheat the oven to 400°F.
2. Cover the chickpeas by 4 to 5 inches of water in a bowl and let sit for 24 hours. Drain thoroughly.
3. Combine the chickpeas, onion, garlic, parsley, lemon zest and juice, cumin, baking soda, salt, black pepper, and cayenne in a food processor. Pulse until coarsely combined. If the mixture is struggling to come together, add a bit of water, but no more than 2 tablespoons. (The mixture

will fall apart when cooking if there's too much liquid.) If water is added, stir in the chickpea flour. Adjust seasonings. Shape into 6 patties (it will be a fairly wet dough).

4. Place the patties on a liberally oiled baking sheet. Bake for 15 to 20 minutes, flipping them once halfway through, until golden and firm.

▶ **PREP AND COOK TIME:** 40 minutes, not including the overnight soak

▶ **VARIATION:** Falafel is traditionally deep-fried, which makes for a richer burger. To deep-fry, in a large, heavy, deep saucepan, heat at least 2 inches of oil to 375°F or until a small test scoop of falafel mixture bubbles instantly. (If you have a FryDaddy, it would come in handy here.) Fry the patties for 6 to 8 minutes, until uniformly browned and firm. Transfer to a paper towel–lined plate or a flattened paper bag to drain of excess oil.

CASHEW-LEEK BURGERS WITH BULGUR AND LENTILS

AMERICA'S TEST KITCHEN, the publishers of *Cooks Illustrated*, the reigning lords of precision cooking applied to everyday food, has a terrific recipe for a veggie burger (available on their subscription Web site) that features lentils, bulgur, cashews—and mayonnaise. I liked the idea, but wanted something that would omit the mayo, because while I'll occasionally make my own mayo, it's not something that I often keep (or want to keep) on hand. I ended up going in a slightly different direction when I discovered that leeks and cashews are an unexpectedly delicious pair. In most burgers, I prefer whole-wheat bread crumbs to white ones, but in this burger I especially recommend them.

▶ MAKES SIX 4-INCH BURGERS

⅓ cup brown or red lentils

⅓ cup bulgur

4 tablespoons olive oil

8 cremini mushrooms, thinly sliced

2 medium leeks, cleaned and finely chopped (see page 41)

1 teaspoon dried thyme

2 garlic cloves, minced

1 tablespoon tomato paste

½ cup toasted cashews

2 eggs

1 teaspoon salt

¼ teaspoon freshly ground black pepper

1 cup toasted bread crumbs

1. Pick through the lentils and rinse thoroughly. Bring the lentils and at least 2 cups water to a boil in a small saucepan. Cover, reduce the heat, and simmer for 20 to 25 minutes, until the lentils are cooked and beginning to fall apart. Transfer to a baking sheet or mixing bowl to cool.

2. Meanwhile, bring ⅔ cup water to a boil. Stir in the bulgur with a pinch of salt, cover, and remove from the heat. Let stand for about 7 minutes, until all the liquid is absorbed.

3. Preheat the oven to 375°F.

4. Heat 1 tablespoon of the oil in a sauté pan over medium heat. Add the mushrooms and cook until they release their moisture and it evaporates, 8 to 10 minutes. Transfer to a large mixing bowl and wipe out the sauté pan.

5. Heat 1 tablespoon of the remaining oil in the sauté pan over medium heat. Add the leeks and thyme and cook, stirring frequently, until the leeks are completely softened and beginning to caramelize, 15 to 20 minutes. Stir in the garlic and tomato paste and cook for 2 minutes longer. Transfer to the bowl with the mushrooms and stir to mix.

6. Combine half of the lentils, half of the bulgur, and half of the leek mixture with the cashews, eggs, salt, and pepper in a food processor. Pulse until uniformly puréed but still slightly chunky. Add the puréed mixture and the remaining lentils and bulgur to the remaining leek mixture in the bowl. Work in the bread crumbs. Shape the mixture into 6 patties.

7. In a large oven-safe skillet or nonstick sauté pan, heat the remaining 2 tablespoons oil over medium-high heat. When hot, add the patties and cook until browned on each side, 6 to 10 minutes total. Transfer the pan to the oven and bake for 12 to 15 minutes, until the burgers are firm and cooked through.

▶ PREP AND COOK TIME: 1 hour

HOW TO
CLean Leeks

Leeks are notorious for having bits of sand and dirt lodged throughout, and there are many ways to clean them. One popular method is to slice off the roots and then quarter the leeks lengthwise from the root end to a few inches into the dark green parts (the leek is still in one piece, connected from the top). Pull the leeks open, blossom-like, and gently rub their insides under running water to rid them of dirt.

My preferred method—which more thoroughly cleans and also alleviates the tedious task of chopping wet vegetables—is to chop them before cleaning, cover them with cold water in a large bowl, and swish them around with your hands to dislodge the dirt. Change the water and repeat. Drain in a sieve or colander.

Fava Bean Burgers

THIS BURGER CALLS for dried or canned fava beans (also known as broad beans) rather than fresh ones. Canned and reconstituted favas don't have the vibrant green color of their fresh counterparts, but the flavor is familiarly ripe and slightly sour, here balanced out with chickpeas and then finished with a medley of fresh herbs. Health food stores carry dried favas (you can save yourself some time by buying them pre-shelled), but to find canned, you'll probably need to hunt them down at a specialty grocery or Middle Eastern grocery, if your city has one.

▶ MAKES SIX 4-INCH BURGERS

3 tablespoons olive oil

1 onion, diced

1½ cups cooked fava beans (see headnote)

1 cup cooked chickpeas

½ cup toasted walnuts, coarsely chopped

2 eggs, beaten

2 tablespoons chopped fresh chives

2 tablespoons chopped fresh parsley

2 tablespoons coarsely chopped fresh basil

¾ teaspoon salt

¼ teaspoon freshly ground black pepper

1½ cups toasted bread crumbs

1. Preheat the oven to 375°F.

2. Heat 1 tablespoon of the oil in a sauté pan over medium heat. Add the onion and cook until translucent, 8 to 10 minutes.

3. In a food processor, combine the onion with the fava beans, chickpeas, and walnuts. Process until coarsely combined. Transfer the mixture to a mixing bowl and mix in the eggs, chives, parsley, basil, salt, and pepper. Fold in the bread crumbs. Adjust seasonings. Shape into 6 patties.

4. In a large oven-safe skillet or non-stick sauté pan heat the remaining 2 tablespoons oil over medium-high heat. When hot, add the patties and cook until browned on each side, 6 to 10 minutes total. Transfer the pan to the oven and bake for 12 to 15 minutes, until the burgers are firm and cooked through.

▶ PREP AND COOK TIME: 25 minutes

FAVA BEAN BURGER

QUINOA, RED BEAN, AND WALNUT BURGER

QUINOA, RED BEAN, AND WALNUT BURGERS Ⓥ ⒼⒻ

QUINOA IS A complete protein (a protein that itself contains all the necessary amino acids for our dietary needs) and a valuable grain to keep in your pantry. Its grassy flavor, which I'm not crazy about on its own, is a perfect component in this burger, with the scallions and ginger offering a clean, slightly spicy finish.

▶ MAKES SIX 4-INCH BURGERS

½ cup quinoa, rinsed thoroughly

1 small potato (4 to 5 ounces), peeled and chopped into 1-inch pieces

3 tablespoons olive oil

1 bunch scallions, including an inch of the green parts, thinly sliced

½ cup roughly chopped fresh parsley

2 tablespoons minced fresh ginger

1½ cups cooked red beans

½ cup roughly chopped toasted walnuts

½ teaspoon salt

Juice of ½ lemon

2 tablespoons Pomegranate-Sesame Sauce (page 157)

1. Bring 1 cup water to boil in a small saucepan and add the quinoa. Reduce to a simmer, cover, and cook for 10 to 12 minutes, until the water is absorbed. Let stand for 5 minutes.

2. Meanwhile, steam or boil the potato until tender. Mash with a fork.

3. Heat 1 tablespoon of the oil in a medium skillet over medium heat. Add the scallions and cook just until fragrant, 1 to 2 minutes. Add the parsley and ginger and cook until fragrant, about 30 seconds.

4. In a large bowl, combine the cooked quinoa, cooked potato, parsley-scallion mixture, red beans, and walnuts with a potato masher or your hands. Add the salt and lemon juice. Shape into 6 patties.

5. In a large oven-safe skillet or nonstick sauté pan, heat the remaining 2 tablespoons oil over medium-high heat. When hot, add the patties and spoon 1 teaspoon pomegranate sauce on top of each. Cook until the bottoms are browned, 4 to 5 minutes. Flip and cook the other sides until crisped and slightly firmed, 4 to 5 minutes more.

▶ PREP AND COOK TIME: 30 minutes

RED LENTIL AND CELERY ROOT BURGERS ⓥ

RED LENTILS HAVE a subtler, slightly sweeter flavor and less structure when cooked than the dark green French lentils. Celery root, also known as celeriac, offsets them here with a lovely, clean finish. Celeriac has the flavor of celery but the texture of what I imagine a starch-less potato would have. Look for one that is firm; to prepare for cooking, simply cut off all the dark brown exterior with a sturdy, sharp knife.

▶ **MAKES SIX 4-INCH BURGERS**

1 cup red lentils

1 celery root, peeled and cut into ½-inch dice

3 tablespoons olive oil

1 medium onion, diced

1 tablespoon fresh or ½ teaspoon dried thyme

¼ cup dry red wine

2 tablespoons roughly chopped fresh parsley

¾ teaspoon salt

½ teaspoon freshly ground black pepper

1½ cups fresh bread crumbs (see Note)

1. Preheat the oven to 375°F.

2. Pick through the lentils and rinse thoroughly. Bring the lentils and at least 2 cups water to a boil in a small saucepan. Cover, reduce the heat, and simmer for 20 to 25 minutes, until the lentils are cooked and beginning to fall apart. Transfer to a baking sheet or mixing bowl to cool.

3. In a medium sauté pan, cover the celery root with cold water. Bring to a boil over high heat. Reduce the heat and simmer until the celery root is fork tender, 10 to 15 minutes. Drain and place in the bowl of a food processor with half of the cooked lentils. Pulse until combined but still slightly chunky.

4. In the pan (just wipe out the pan the celery root was cooked in), heat 1 tablespoon of the oil over medium heat. Add the onion and the dried thyme (if using dried instead of fresh). Sauté until the onion is lightly browned, 10 to 12 minutes. If using fresh thyme, add it now and stir for 30 seconds, until fragrant. Deglaze the pan with the red wine and cook

RED LENTIL AND CELERY ROOT BURGER

until most of the liquid has evaporated, about 2 minutes.

5. In a mixing bowl, combine the remaining lentils, the celery root mixture, onion mixture, parsley, salt, and pepper. Fold in the bread crumbs. Let stand for 10 minutes. Adjust seasonings. Shape into 6 patties.

6. In an oven-safe skillet, heat the remaining 2 tablespoons oil over medium-high heat. When hot, add the patties and cook until browned on each side, 6 to 10 minutes total. Transfer the pan to the oven and bake for 12 to 15 minutes, until the burgers are firm and cooked through.

NOTE: The advantage of using fresh—rather than toasted—bread crumbs here is that they give the burgers a bit more heft and don't impart the flavor of toasted crumbs. To make fresh crumbs, cut off the crusts, tear the bread into small pieces, and pulse in a food processor. One slice of bread typically yields about ½ cup of fresh bread crumbs.

▶ PREP AND COOK TIME: 45 minutes

Baked Quinoa Burgers

QUINOA, ONCE BAKED, gives these burgers a delicious crunch. Because quinoa cooks so quickly, they can be ready to go in the time it takes for the oven to preheat. Take your pick between the pepper flakes or nutmeg depending on whether you'd like a touch of heat or a slightly floral note. I rarely make it to condiments with these, opting instead to eat them completely unadorned.

▶ **MAKES SIX 4-INCH BURGERS**

1 cup quinoa

5 ounces spinach, fresh or frozen

1 small shallot, minced

2 garlic cloves, minced

1 egg, beaten

3 tablespoons all-purpose flour

1 teaspoon baking powder

1 teaspoon sea salt

¼ teaspoon freshly ground black pepper

Pinch red pepper flakes or freshly grated nutmeg

1. Preheat the oven to 400°F. Line a baking sheet with parchment paper.

2. Thoroughly rinse the quinoa. Bring the quinoa and 2 cups water to a boil in a small saucepan. Reduce the heat and add a pinch of salt. Cover and simmer for 10 to 15 minutes, until the water is absorbed. Transfer to a mixing bowl and allow to cool slightly.

3. Meanwhile, prepare the spinach: If using fresh spinach, steam it for 3 to 4 minutes over an inch of simmering water or blanch it for 30 seconds in a pot of boiling salted water. Transfer to an ice bath to halt the cooking. Squeeze dry and finely chop. If using frozen spinach, allow it to thaw and then squeeze dry.

4. Combine the cooked quinoa and spinach with the shallot, garlic, egg, flour, baking powder, salt, black pepper, and red pepper or nutmeg. Shape into 6 patties and place on the prepared baking sheet.

5. Bake for 15 to 20 minutes, rotating the baking sheet halfway through, until golden brown and firm.

▶ **PREP AND COOK TIME:** 30 minutes

PUB GRUB
VEGGIE BURGER

PUB GRUB VEGGIE BURGERS

WHAT'S A COOKBOOK without at least one calorie bomb? I've had many veggie burgers at pubs and restaurants that taste just a little bit *too* good. When I probed the waitress at one restaurant for what *exactly* makes it so good, what she told me—a combination of beans, cheese, chili powder— didn't seem to completely add up. I finally figured out the secret of the pub veggie burger: like most everything else on a pub menu, it was deep-fried. (Do note my restraint in frying these in only an inch of oil rather than fully submerging them. If you want to go whole hog, see page 143 for a few guidelines.)

▶ MAKES EIGHT 4-INCH BURGERS

1 onion, chopped

3 eggs

1½ cups cooked black beans

1½ cups cooked chickpeas

1 teaspoon chili powder

1 teaspoon salt

1½ cups panko crumbs

1 cup grated nice-melting cheese such as pepper Jack, Muenster, mozzarella, or Fontina cheese

¼ cup chopped fresh parsley

Peanut, canola, or vegetable oil for shallow frying

1. Combine the onion, eggs, beans, chickpeas, chili powder, and salt in a food processor and pulse until combined. Transfer to a mixing bowl and fold in the panko, cheese, and parsley. Shape into 8 patties.

2. Heat 1 inch of oil in a deep skillet or sauté pan over medium-high heat. Cook the patties in batches to avoid crowding, turning once, until uniformly browned, 8 to 12 minutes total. Transfer to a paper towel–lined plate or flattened paper bag to drain of excess oil.

▶ PREP AND COOK TIME: 20 minutes

3

VEGETABLE BURGERS

THIS IS WHAT it's all about, isn't it? A veggie burger is nothing if not a celebration of vegetables, and these recipes are a veritable Pride Parade of what's typically relegated to the perimeters of Hamburger Nation. I have yet to encounter a vegetable that has disappointed me in a veggie burger, even though I sometimes have had to finesse certain vegetables with additional ingredients in order to bring them to their full potential. Here are a few basic principles to observe when making burgers with vegetables.

✷ COOK FIRST TO SOFTEN AND FOR FLAVOR: A vegetable that is firm in its raw state needs to be cooked beforehand by roasting, sautéing, parboiling, or steaming (see below for a few examples).

Additionally, many vegetables—onions and carrots, for example—benefit from being cooked before mixing into veggie burgers to temper their sharpness and concentrate their flavor.

✳ WATCH MOISTURE LEVELS: Vegetables contain a great deal of liquid. By cooking them before adding them to a burger mixture, you're cooking off some of that liquid. This ensures that moisture won't be released when the burger itself is cooked, which would render it wet and mushy.

✳ EXTEND WITH STARCH: As with all the recipes in this book, no veggie burger is made from a single ingredient. The primary vegetable in each burger needs to be stretched with a starch such as beans, rice, or potatoes in order to be made malleable.

Here are a few guidelines for vegetables that have more involved preparations:

GREENS: Greens such as spinach, chard, and kale need to be cooked and squeezed dry of their liquid before adding to a veggie burger mixture. There are several ways to do this. With all methods, the hot greens can be transferred with tongs or a slotted spoon to an ice bath to halt the cooking and retain the vibrant color of the greens. (Heartier greens like kale and collard greens take longer to cook than more delicate leaves like spinach.)

■ To sauté: Cook the greens in a small amount of oil over medium-low heat until wilted.

■ To steam: Place the greens in a steaming basket set in a small saucepan with 1 inch of simmering water and steam until the greens collapse.

■ To blanch: Cook the greens in a pot of boiling salted water until tender. They will cook very quickly, 30 seconds to 2 minutes, depending on the heartiness of the greens.

LARGE SQUASH: Large squash such as butternut, acorn, and kombucha aren't very pleasant to eat raw, nor are they particularly easy to digest. But squash has a place in many veggie burger recipes because when cooked, it lends an assertive autumnal flavor and a soft, slightly binding texture. I prefer roasting squash as opposed to boiling it, partially because the unused cooking water retains some of the squash's flavor, but mostly because I love when my apartment fills with the delicious aroma.

- **To roast:** Cut the squash in half through the stem. Rub with a bit of oil and place, cut-side down, on a greased baking sheet. Roast in a 450°F oven, flipping twice so that the squash finishes cut-side down, for 25 to 45 minutes, until the squash can be effortlessly pierced with a sharp knife at its thickest area. When cool, trim away the peel with a paring knife or vegetable peeler and scoop out the seeds.
- **To boil:** Peel the squash, scoop out the seeds, and chop the flesh into 1-inch pieces. Cook in a pot of salted boiling water for 12 to 20 minutes, until tender. Drain thoroughly.

BEETS: Freshly cooked beets will be a treat if you're used to the canned variety that shows up in salad bars. Beets can be roasted, steamed, or boiled, the latter being the quickest method. For all methods, save peeling for after cooking; it's much easier.

- **To roast:** Place the beets on a square of aluminum foil and rub with 1 teaspoon olive oil. Wrap tightly in the foil and roast in a 400°F oven for 45 minutes to 1 hour, until completely tender.
- **To steam:** Place the beets in a steaming basket set in a small pot or saucepan with 1 to 2 inches of simmering water. Steam for 25 to 45 minutes, until the beets are completely tender. You will need to add additional water every 10 minutes.
- **To boil:** Cook the beets in a pot of salted boiling water, partially covered, for 20 to 35 minutes, until completely tender.

MUSHROOMS: While not technically a vegetable (they are rather the outgrowth of a fungus), no other ingredient makes the bold, hearty statement in veggie burgers that mushrooms do. They add chewy texture and distinctive earthy flavor. It's important that the mushrooms be cooked before adding them to a burger mixture: they contain a significant amount of water, and unless you cook it out beforehand, it will be released inside the burger and make it soggy.

- **To sauté:** Most mushrooms are best sautéed; for small mushrooms like cremini, shiitake, and button mushrooms, they should be sliced about ¼ inch thick. Heat a bit of oil in a sauté pan over medium-high heat. Add the sliced mushrooms in a single layer. Cook, flipping occasionally, until they release their liquid—suddenly, the sauté pan will have a pool of gray water in it—and then let the water cook off. They will have shrunken up slightly and will be browned on each side.

- **To roast:** Some cooks advocate roasting mushrooms (as I do in the Tortilla-Crusted Stuffed Portobello Burgers, page 69). Simply layer the mushrooms on an ungreased baking sheet and roast in a 400° F preheated oven until the mushrooms' liquid has been released and cooked off. With smaller mushrooms like shiitakes and cremini mushrooms you can go one step further: roast them at a low temperature until they completely dry out. These chewy mushroom "chips" are wonderful as a condiment in all types of pastas and salads.

BeST PORTOBELLO BURGERS Ⓥ Ⓖ

NO MATTER HOW many variations on a hamburger a typical burger joint menu offers, the prevailing way of preparing portobello mushroom burgers in restaurants is to drench them in cheap, cloyingly sweet balsamic vinegar. The first thing I realized when I began developing my portobello burger was that the mushroom needed a savory marinade. Enter miso paste, the fermented soybean paste that is the basis of miso soup and soy sauce. For years I've been adding miso to salad dressings and marinades—why not use it to season a portobello burger? The results blew me away. Miso offers a warm, nuanced saltiness that perfectly complements the natural earthiness of the mushroom.

▶ MAKES 4 BURGERS

4 medium portobello mushrooms
3 tablespoons olive oil
1 tablespoon rice vinegar
2 teaspoons miso paste (GF)
½ teaspoon freshly ground black pepper

1. Trim off the stems of the mushrooms and scrape out the gills with a spoon. Place the caps in a large baking dish or mixing bowl.
2. In a small bowl, whisk together the oil, vinegar, miso, and pepper. Pour over the mushrooms and, using your hands, toss to ensure that all the mushrooms are evenly coated. Marinate for at least 15 minutes or up to 2 hours.
3. Heat a large sauté pan over medium-high heat. Add the mushrooms, rounded tops down, and cook for 10 to 15 minutes total, flipping them halfway through. The mushrooms should be tender in the thick center. Watch for them to release their juices, and then for most of the liquid to cook off the pan.

GRILL METHOD: Prepare a medium fire over a charcoal or gas grill. Grill the mushrooms over an open flame for a total of 10 to 12 minutes, beginning with the rounded top down and flipping halfway through.

▶ Variations

■ **STUFFED PORTOBELLO BURGERS WITH CHEESE:** Mash together 1 cup cooked brown rice, ½ cup red or black beans, and a generous pinch of salt. Spread this mixture into the cups of the cooked mushrooms and then lay a piece of mozzarella, Monterey Jack, queso fresco, white Cheddar, or your favorite soy cheese over the mixture. Place under the broiler until the cheese melts. Serve open-faced on a grilled slab of ciabatta or other airy bread.

■ **SESAME SEAWEED PORTOBELLO BURGERS:** Add ½ teaspoon toasted sesame oil and ¼ teaspoon wasabi powder to the marinade. Top the cooked burger with a spoonful of prepared seaweed salad and a sprinkling of sesame seeds and serve on a soft, toasted sesame bun.

■ **SPINACH AND CHEESE PORTOBELLO BURGERS:** Martha Rose Shulman of the *New York Times* recommends melting a piece of Gruyère cheese over the top of a cooked mushroom underneath a broiler or in the pan, and fitting a small mound of blanched, chopped spinach between the hamburger bun and the cavity of the mushroom. This is delicious on Whole-Wheat Burger Buns (page 115).

■ **CALIFORNIA PORTOBELLO BURGERS:** On a Basic Burger Bun (page 111), place a cooked mushroom over a layer of avocado slices and a few splashes of hot sauce or Sriracha, and top with Quick-Pickled Red Onions (page 155) and a few pieces of lettuce.

▶ **PREP AND COOK TIME:** 30 minutes

BEET AND BROWN RICE BURGERS Ⓥ ⒢

**RED WINE VINEGAR is the secret
ingredient here, bringing a
slightly floral and acidic note
to the burger. "Searing" this
delicate burger on high heat at
the beginning of the cooking
process is important; the crust
that forms is what helps the
burger keep its shape. I like
to top this one with the Quick-
Pickled Red Onions (page 155)
and a handful of fresh arugula.**

▶ **MAKES SIX 4-INCH BURGERS**

3 medium beets, scrubbed clean, ends
 trimmed

4 tablespoons olive oil

1 red onion, diced

½ teaspoon salt

1 tablespoon red wine vinegar

1½ cups cooked black or red beans

1 cup cooked brown rice

2 tablespoons chopped fresh parsley

Freshly ground black pepper

1. Using the large holes of a box grater
   or the grater blade of your food processor, grate the beets. (It's not necessary to peel them first.)

2. In a large, lidded sauté pan, heat 2
   tablespoons of the oil over medium
   heat. Add the onion and cook until
   it softens and begins to look translucent, 6 to 8 minutes. Add the beets
   and salt and toss to combine. Cover
   and cook for 10 to 12 minutes, until
   the beets are completely softened.
   Add the vinegar, toss to combine,
   and scrape up the browned bits from
   the pan with a wooden spoon. Set
   aside to cool slightly.

3. In a mixing bowl, coarsely mash the
   beans with a potato masher or fork.
   Fold in the beet mixture, the rice, parsley, and black pepper to taste. Adjust
   seasonings. Shape into six patties, flattening to a ½-inch thickness.

4. In a sauté pan, heat the remaining 2
   tablespoons oil over high heat. Add
   the patties, in batches if necessary to
   avoid crowding. They should sizzle—
   this creates a nice crust. Cook for 1

*Way too many beets.
Try one the size of your fist or sl. bigger*

minute. Reduce the heat to medium and cook for 2 or 3 minutes. Carefully flip the burgers and cook until browned and firm, 4 to 5 minutes longer.

▶ PREP AND COOK TIME: 20 minutes

BEET AND BROWN RICE BURGER

THaI CaRROT BURGeRS

THIS RECIPE CALLS for just a small amount of peanut butter. You'll need to use the natural, minimally processed kind that is made to order with a peanut butter machine at some grocery stores. If you are accustomed to Skippy, you'll find that natural peanut butter is alarmingly dense, and that its natural oils collect at the top of the container. Be sure to store natural peanut butter in the refrigerator. If you can't find it, buy something that is as unadulterated as possible (organic, low-salt, definitely no sweeteners). Red Cabbage Slaw (page 127) goes nicely with these burgers, either as a side or served directly on the burgers, as does julienned cabbage that's been tossed in a bit of rice vinegar and salt.

▶ MAKES FOUR 6-INCH BURGERS

3 tablespoons olive oil

1 bunch scallions, including 1 inch into the dark green parts, thinly sliced

3 garlic cloves, minced

2-inch piece fresh ginger, grated

1 serrano chile pepper, finely chopped (seeded or not, depending on your personal heat threshold)

4 cups grated carrots (about 8 medium carrots)

1 teaspoon salt

1 teaspoon ground coriander

¾ teaspoon ground turmeric

½ teaspoon ground cinnamon

2 egg whites

2 tablespoons natural peanut butter

Juice of ½ lime

¼ cup roughly chopped cilantro

½ cup toasted bread crumbs

1. Preheat the oven to 375°F.
2. Heat a large lidded sauté pan over medium heat. Add 1 tablespoon of the oil. When hot, add the scallions and cook just until they begin to soften, about 2 minutes. Add the garlic, ginger, and chile pepper and stir for 30 seconds, until fragrant. Stir in the carrots, salt, coriander,

turmeric, and cinnamon. Cover and cook for 6 to 8 minutes, until the carrots are soft but not mushy.

3. In a mixing bowl, whisk together the egg whites, peanut butter, and lime juice. Stir in the carrot mixture and the cilantro. Fold in the bread crumbs. Let sit for about 10 minutes, allowing the crumbs to absorb some of the liquid. Adjust seasonings. Shape into 4 patties.

4. In an oven-safe skillet or nonstick sauté pan, heat the remaining 2 tablespoons oil over medium-high heat. When hot, add the patties and cook until browned on each side, 4 to 6 minutes total. Transfer the pan to the oven and bake for 12 to 15 minutes, until the burgers are firm and cooked through.

▶ PREP AND COOK TIME: 30 minutes

THAI CARROT BURGER

MUSHROOM BURGERS WITH BARLEY ⓥ ⓖⒻ

THIS BURGER, BASED in part on the fortifying soup, is simple and delicious and abundant in mushroom flavor. Substitute other mushroom varieties, such as oyster mushrooms or plain button mushrooms. The combination of mushrooms and barley makes for a deliciously chewy veggie burger.

▶ MAKES 6 BURGERS

1 small potato, peeled and cut into ½-inch pieces

3 tablespoons olive oil, divided

1 portobello mushroom

12 cremini mushrooms

10 shiitake mushrooms

½ teaspoon dried thyme

2 tablespoons basalmic vinegar

1 cup cooked barley

½ teaspoon salt

¼ teaspoon freshly ground black pepper

1. Steam or boil the potato until tender. Mash with a fork.

2. Trim off the stem of the portobello mushroom and scoop out the gills. Chop into ½-inch pieces. Thinly slice the cremini and shiitake mushrooms

3. Preheat oven to 375° F.

4. Heat 1 tablespoon of the oil over medium heat. Cook the portobello mushrooms and dried thyme for 6 to 8 minutes, until the mushrooms begin to soften and sweat. Add the cremini and shiitake. Cook for 10 minutes, until the mushrooms have sweat off their moisture and it has dried up in the pan. Deglaze with the vinegar.

5. Transfer mushrooms to a food processor and coarsely purée. (Alternatively, chop the mushrooms finely by hand.) Combine the mushroom mixture with the potato, barley, salt, and pepper in a mixing bowl. Shape into 6 patties.

6. In a large oven-safe skillet or nonstick sauté pan heat the remaining 2 tablespoons oil over medium-high heat. When hot, add the patties and cook until browned on each side, 6 to 10 minutes total. Transfer the pan to the oven and bake for 12 to 15 minutes, until the burgers are firm and cooked through.

▶ PREP AND COOK TIME: 30 minutes

MUSHROOM BURGER
WITH BARLEY

BEET "TARTARE" ⓖⓕ

WHO ELSE BUT a French chef would have the idea to serve beets like raw beef? The inspiration for this surprising beet "tartare" burger—named more for its presentation than the method, since we *are* cooking the beets—comes from Chef Pascal Bonhomme of Pascalou, a bistro on Manhattan's Upper East Side, where I have worked. You'll need 4-ounce ramekins, though you can also cook in batches with fewer ramekins or using a metal ½-cup measuring cup. This is good with any variety of beets— red, gold, or Chioggia—but you'll only get the true "tartare" effect with the dark purple ones.

▶ **MAKES 5 OR 6 "BURGERS"**

5 medium beets, scrubbed clean and trimmed of stems and fibrous roots

1 teaspoon olive oil

1 egg white

1 small shallot, minced

2 teaspoons sherry vinegar

2 teaspoons minced fresh tarragon

1 teaspoon potato starch or cornstarch

6 tablespoons crumbled goat cheese

Freshly ground black pepper

Additional fresh tarragon leaves and minced shallot for garnish

1. Roast the beets: Preheat the oven to 400°F. Place the beets on a square of aluminum foil and rub with the oil. Wrap tightly in the foil. Roast for 45 minutes to 1 hour, until completely tender. Cool completely. Peel the beets and chop into small dice— approximately ⅛-inch.

2. In a mixing bowl, whisk together the egg white, shallot, vinegar, tarragon, and potato starch. Fold in the diced beets.

3. Line the bottom of each (4-ounce) ramekins with a small circle of parchment paper. Using your fingers, grease the sides of each ramekin and its parchment with a bit of olive oil. Pack each ramekin with the beet mixture, leveling off the top for a flat surface. Depending on the size of your beets, you will have enough to fill either 5 or 6 ramekins.

BEET "TARTARE"

4. Cover each ramekin with microwave-safe plastic wrap and microwave for 1 minute until firmed. Alternatively, steam the ramekins: Bring ½ inch water to a simmer in a stockpot or saucepan with a colander or steaming basket insert. In batches if necessary, add the ramekins, cover, and steam the beet "burgers" for 3 minutes, until the mixture congeals.

5. Let the ramekins cool to room temperature. (At this stage they can be refrigerated for up to 2 days.) Run a thin, sharp knife around the perimeter of a ramekin to loosen the beet mixture and invert onto a serving plate. It will come out in a single patty-shaped piece. Remove the parchment. Repeat with the remaining ramekins.

6. To serve, top each "burger" with 1 tablespoon of goat cheese and black pepper to taste. Garnish with a few sprigs of tarragon and some minced shallot.

▶ **PREP AND COOK TIME:** 1 hour
▶ **DO AHEAD:** Roast beets

TORTILLa-CRUSTED STUFFED PORTOBELLO BURGERS GF

THIS BURGER IS inspired by the indulgent, unique veggie burger at Alias, a restaurant on Manhattan's Lower East Side: two portobello mushrooms sandwich a thick slice of queso blanco and a layer of puréed black beans and are then crusted with panko and deep-fried. I use tortilla chip crumbs instead of panko and have cut back a bit with the cheese and the deep-frying, but this is still a burger worth writing home about. It's great on a big, soft bun and topped with pico de gallo and fresh avocado slices. Use the smallest portobello mushrooms you can find; if they are too large, they become unwieldy.

▶ MAKES 4 BURGERS

8 small portobello mushrooms

3 cups plain tortilla chips

1 cup cooked black beans

4 ounces queso blanco cheese (about ½ cup)

2 tablespoons roughly chopped cilantro

1 teaspoon salt

3 tablespoons white rice flour or all-purpose flour

2 eggs, beaten

¼ cup olive oil

1. Preheat the oven to 400°F. Lightly grease a baking sheet.
2. Trim the stems from the mushrooms and scrape out the gills with a spoon. Place the caps rounded sides up on the prepared baking sheet. Roast, flipping every 5 minutes, for 15 to 20 minutes, until the mushrooms are tender and have given off most of their liquid. Let cool.
3. Reduce the oven temperature to 350°F.
4. In food processor, pulse the tortilla chips until uniformly ground. Transfer the crumbs to a shallow bowl and

set aside. Add the black beans, queso fresco, cilantro, and ½ teaspoon of the salt to the processor and purée.

5. To assemble the burgers: Sandwich 2 heaping tablespoons of the bean mixture between 2 roasted mushrooms, rounded sides out. Repeat to make 4 burgers.

6. Combine the flour and remaining ½ teaspoon salt in a second shallow bowl. Place the beaten eggs in a third shallow bowl. Dredge each burger in the flour, then the egg, letting the excess drip off, and then coat with tortilla crumbs.

7. In an oven-proof skillet or nonstick sauté pan, heat the oil over medium heat. When hot, add the burgers and cook until golden on each side, 6 to 10 minutes total. Transfer the pan to the oven and bake for 10 to 12 minutes, until the burger exteriors are uniformly browned and the breading fully firmed.

▶ PREP AND COOK TIME: 45 minutes, including cooling time

Baked Cauliflower Burgers

IF YOU CAN get a cauliflower at the farmers' market in season (fall is peak season, beginning in October) you'll find that its natural sweetness is much more readily apparent than in the plastic wrapped ones found year-round at the supermarket. Here, capers and Dijon mustard highlight mellow cauliflower's subtle flavor. Serve with a slice of Swiss or Gruyère cheese for something richer; or for a lighter lunch, season with a squeeze of lemon, a sprinkling of sea salt, and a few grinds of black pepper and serve on a big, fluffy kaiser roll.

▶ MAKES SIX 4-INCH BURGERS

1 head cauliflower, cut into large florets

3 tablespoons Dijon mustard

2 tablespoons potato starch

2 eggs

Squeeze of fresh lemon juice

¼ cup roughly chopped parsley

2 tablespoons capers, drained, rinsed, and roughly chopped

¼ teaspoon red pepper flakes

1¼ teaspoons salt

1½ cups toasted bread crumbs

¼ cup finely grated Parmesan

1. Preheat the oven to 350°F. Line a baking sheet with parchment paper.

2. Place the cauliflower in a steaming basket set in a small saucepan with 1 inch of simmering water, cover, and steam for 8 to 10 minutes, until the cauliflower can be effortlessly pierced with a knife. Cool slightly on a baking sheet or cutting board.

3. In a food processor, purée two-thirds of the steamed cauliflower with the mustard, potato starch, eggs, and lemon juice until smooth. Transfer to a large mixing bowl.

4. Chop the remaining cauliflower into ⅛- to ¼-inch pieces (or pulse in a food processor until roughly chopped). Add to the puréed mixture. Stir in the parsley, capers, red pepper flakes, and ½ teaspoon of the salt. Fold in 1 cup of the bread crumbs. Adjust seasonings. Shape into 6 patties.

5. Combine the remaining ½ cup bread crumbs, remaining ¾ teaspoon salt, and the Parmesan on a plate. Gently dredge the patties in the crumbs so they are coated on both sides and the edges. Place on the prepared baking sheet. Bake for 20 to 25 minutes, flipping once halfway through, until the burgers are firm and uniformly browned.

▶ **PREP AND COOK TIME:** 30 minutes

▶ **VARIATION: BAKED ROMANESCO BURGERS**

Romanesco, a centuries-old vegetable that has been reappearing at farmers' markets with more frequency over the past few years, is a hybrid of cauliflower and broccoli. It has a sea-green color and its shape resembles something out of a science fiction movie, with florets of spiraling domes. You can substitute 1 head of romanesco for the cauliflower in this recipe. It steams in roughly the same amount of time as cauliflower.

BAKED CAULIFLOWER BURGER

BUTTERNUT SQUASH, BLACK BEAN, AND CHESTNUT BURGERS Ⓥ

THIS HEARTY BURGER is inspired by a delicious burrito I once had, save the addition of chestnuts, which offers a sweet dimension suggestive of Thanksgiving pies. A slice of soy cheese or mozzarella cheese really brings all the flavors together. Since the recipe only calls for half of a butternut squash, you might as well roast the other half at the same time and reserve it for soup.

▶ **MAKES SIX 4-INCH BURGERS**

1 onion

½ medium butternut squash, split lengthwise from the stem

2 tablespoons plus 1 teaspoon olive oil, divided

5 ounces spinach, fresh or frozen

1½ cups cooked black beans

½ cup roasted chestnuts, chopped (see note)

1 teaspoon salt

3 tablespoons vital wheat gluten

1½ cups toasted bread crumbs

1. Preheat the oven to 400°F. Line a baking sheet with foil.

2. Peel and quarter the onion along the stem, leaving the base attached to each quarter so that it holds its shape. Rub the onion and the squash with 1 teaspoon of the oil, and arrange on the baking sheet, with the squash lying flat. Roast for 25 to 35 minutes, flipping the squash twice so that it finishes facedown, until both the onion and the squash are completely tender. If the onion begins to burn while the squash is still cooking, remove it from the pan. Cool until safe to handle.

3. Reduce the oven temperature to 375°F.

4. Scoop out the seeds and peel the skin off the squash. Trim the base from the onions. Pulse the onions, squash, and chestnuts in a food processor just until combined. (Alternatively, chop the onions and chestnuts by hand and mash the squash with a fork or potato masher).

5. Meanwhile, prepare the spinach: If using fresh spinach, steam it for 3 to

4 minutes over an inch of simmering water or blanch it for 30 seconds in a pot of boiling salted water. Transfer to an ice bath to halt the cooking. Squeeze dry and finely chop. If using frozen spinach, allow it to thaw. Squeeze dry and finely chop.

6. Mash the black beans with a fork or potato masher in a large mixing bowl. Fold in the spinach, squash mixture, and salt. Fold in the vital wheat gluten and bread crumbs. Adjust seasonings, then let stand for 15 minutes. Shape into 6 patties.

7. In a large oven-safe skillet or non-stick sauté pan heat the remaining oil over medium-high heat. When hot, add the patties and cook until browned on each side, 6 to 10 minutes total. Transfer the pan to the oven and bake for 12 to 15 minutes, until the burgers are firm and cooked through.

NOTE: Roasted chestnuts are easy to find during the holidays. Otherwise you'll have better luck at a specialty grocery. Don't buy the canned chestnuts that are submerged in water. You want either the ones that are jarred, which are not submerged in any liquid, or vacuum-sealed.

▶ PREP AND COOK TIME: 1 hour

SPINACH-CHICKPEA BURGER

SPINACH-CHICKPEA BURGERS ⒼⒻ

THIS IS ONE of my favorite veggie burgers. It has everything I want: hearty chickpeas, fortifying spinach, a hint of nutty toasted cumin seeds, and final finish of fresh lemon. It's also very easy! As with most burgers in this book, be sure to reserve a portion of the beans and mash them by hand, rather than blitzing all of them in the food processor, as this gives the burger texture. I like to serve them accompanied by traditional burger fixings: lettuce, tomato, and mustard. Served with Gluten-Free Burger Bread (page 122), it's a totally gluten-free meal.

▶ **MAKES FIVE 4-INCH BURGERS**

2 tablespoons plus 1 teaspoon olive oil

1 teaspoon toasted cumin seeds

5 ounces fresh spinach

1½ cups cooked chickpeas

2 eggs

Juice of ½ lemon

1 teaspoon salt

⅓ cup chickpea flour (see Note), or more if needed

1. Heat 1 teaspoon of the oil in a medium skillet. Add the cumin seeds and spinach and cook, tossing with tongs, until the spinach is completely wilted, 2 or 3 minutes. Transfer to a heatproof plate and allow to cool until safe to handle. Drain if necessary, wrap in a towel, and squeeze out as much liquid as possible. Chop finely.

2. Combine 1¼ cups of the chickpeas, the eggs, lemon juice, and salt in a food processor. Pulse until the mixture resembles a chunky hummus.

3. In a large bowl, combine the spinach with the remaining ¼ cup beans and mash coarsely with a potato masher. Add the bean-egg mixture and stir thoroughly. Fold in the chickpea flour. The mixture should be sticky but somewhat pliable. Add more flour, 1 teaspoon at a time, if too wet, or a bit of water if too dry. Shape into 5 patties.

4. In an oven-safe skillet or nonstick sauté pan, heat the remaining 2 tablespoons oil over medium-high heat. When hot, add the patties and cook until browned on each side, 6

to 10 minutes total. Transfer the pan to the oven and bake for 12 to 15 minutes, until the burgers are firm and cooked through.

NOTE: While it's easy to make your own chickpea flour by grinding dried chickpeas in a spice grinder or blender, it can now be found at most grocery stores—but at a hefty price. It's a standard ingredient in Indian cuisines, used to make a breading batter for *pakoras* and in some flatbreads, and can thus be found readily and less expensively at Indian groceries, where it sometimes called gram flour.

▶ PREP AND COOK TIME: 25 minutes

SWEET POTATO BURGERS WITH LENTILS AND KALE

THIS IS A hearty, nutritious burger. Instead of kale, feel free to substitute chard, beet greens, spinach, or any other hearty leafy greens you might have on hand. Likewise, if you have a leftover roasted sweet potato, use it instead of the steamed potato. The burgers are delicious topped with any of the yogurt sauces (pages 161 and 162).

▶ **MAKES SIX 4-INCH BURGERS**

¾ cup French (green) lentils

1 bunch kale, tough stems removed

1 medium sweet potato (about 8 ounces), peeled and chopped into 1-inch pieces

4 tablespoons olive oil

1 medium onion, diced

1½ teaspoons garam masala

1½ teaspoons curry powder

Pinch of cayenne pepper

3 garlic cloves

2 eggs, beaten

3 tablespoons chopped fresh cilantro

½ teaspoon salt

Squeeze of fresh lime juice

¾ cup toasted bread crumbs

¼ cup almond meal (see Note)

1. Pick through the lentils and rinse thoroughly. Bring the lentils and at least 3 cups water to a boil in a small saucepan. Cover, reduce the heat, and simmer for 15 to 20 minutes, until tender. Drain and then transfer lentils to a large mixing bowl. Coarsely mash them with a potato masher.

2. Meanwhile, steam the kale: Place the kale in a steaming basket set in a saucepan with 1 inch of simmering water, cover, and steam for 5 to 8 minutes, until completely tender. Remove the kale. When cool enough to handle, wrap in a clean kitchen cloth and squeeze out as much liquid as possible. Finely chop and set aside.

3. Place the sweet potato in the steaming basket, adding more water if necessary. Cover and cook for 8 to 10 minutes, until the potato is completely tender. Add the potato to the

lentils, mashing thoroughly with a fork or potato masher.

4. Preheat the oven to 375°F.

5. In a sauté pan, heat 2 tablespoons of the oil over medium heat. Add the onion, garam masala, curry powder, and cayenne and cook until the onion is translucent, 8 to 10 minutes. Add the chopped kale and the garlic. Cook for about 2 minutes, tossing to combine. If a crust has formed on the base of the pan, add 2 tablespoons water and scrape up the browned bits with a wooden spoon.

6. Mix the kale-onion mixture into the lentil mixture. Stir in the eggs, cilantro, salt, and lime juice. Fold in the bread crumbs and almond meal. Adjust seasonings. Shape into 6 patties.

7. In an oven-safe skillet or nonstick sauté pan, heat the remaining 2 tablespoons oil over medium-high heat. When hot, add the patties and cook until browned on each side, 6 to 10 minutes total. Transfer the pan to the oven and bake for 12 to 15 minutes, until the burgers are firm and cooked through.

NOTE: Almond meal is similar to almond flour. The only difference is that almond flour is made from blanched almonds, where the skins have been removed, and for the purposes of veggie burgers, the two are interchangeable. It's readily available now at grocery stores and Trader Joe's, but if your city has a Middle Eastern shopping area or grocery, you'll find a cheaper, better-quality product there. You can also make your own by grinding up roasted almonds in small batches in a food processor—but be careful not to grind it into a paste.

▶ PREP AND COOK TIME: 45 minutes, including time to cool

SWEET POTATO BURGER
WITH LENTILS AND KALE

CORN BURGER WITH SUN-DRIED
TOMATOES AND GOAT CHEESE

CORN BURGERS WITH SUN-DRIED TOMATOES AND GOAT CHEESE

THIS UTTERLY DELICIOUS burger is part flapjack, part veggie burger. It's too wet to shape into patties—you just drop a big spoonful of the mixture into a hot sauté pan. Try it as a savory breakfast, as the base for a simple salad, or on a crusty wheat roll topped with goat cheese and pico de gallo.

▶ MAKES SIX 5-INCH BURGERS

1½ cups fresh (from about 3 ears) or frozen corn

2 eggs

½ cup stone-ground cornmeal or polenta

¼ cup all-purpose flour

2 teaspoons cornstarch

½ teaspoon baking powder

6 scallions, including 1 inch into the dark green parts, thinly sliced

1 cup oil-packed sun-dried tomatoes, diced

3 ounces goat cheese

½ teaspoon salt

¼ teaspoon freshly ground black pepper

2 tablespoons olive oil

1. Pulse 1 cup of the corn and the eggs in a food processor until the texture of chunky hummus, not completely liquefied.

2. In a mixing bowl, whisk together the cornmeal, flour, cornstarch, and baking powder. Stir in the remaining ½ cup corn, the corn-egg mixture, the scallions, sun-dried tomatoes, salt, and pepper. Crumble the goat cheese over the corn mixture and fold it in. Adjust the seasonings.

3. Heat the oil in a sauté pan over medium heat. Drop the mixture by heaping ¼-cup portions into the hot skillet, pressing gently with a spatula to round them into burger shapes. Cook until golden brown on the bottoms, 4 to 5 minutes (lower the heat if they cook too quickly). Carefully flip and cook until firm and browned, another 4 or 5 minutes.

▶ PREP AND COOK TIME: 30 minutes

CURRIED EGGPLANT AND TOMATO BURGER

CURRIED EGGPLANT AND TOMATO BURGERS Ⓥ ⒼⒻ

CURRY SPICES GIVE these burgers a sweet, complex heat. If you can't find a Japanese eggplant, use a baby eggplant or the smaller Italian eggplant, as most regular-size eggplants have too much water for this recipe. Slather the burgers with Curried Tomato Relish (page 156) and top with a handful of Frizzled Shallots (page 152).

▶ MAKES FOUR 4-INCH BURGERS

1 Japanese eggplant (about 12 ounces)

1 cup cherry tomatoes

1½ cups cooked brown rice

1 small red onion, finely chopped

3 garlic cloves, minced

2 tablespoons roughly chopped cilantro

1 teaspoon curry powder

1 teaspoon garam masala

½ teaspoon molasses

½ teaspoon salt

Pinch of cayenne pepper

1 medium Yukon Gold potato, peeled, steamed, and mashed with a fork

2 teaspoons potato starch

2 tablespoons olive oil

1. Preheat the oven to 450°F. Line a baking sheet with foil.

2. Prick the eggplant all over with a fork. Place the eggplant and tomatoes on the prepared baking sheet. Roast, stirring the tomatoes and flipping the eggplant every 5 minutes. After about 20 minutes, the tomatoes should be done—they will begin to shrivel but still be supple (as they cool off, they will exude some additional liquid). Carefully remove the tomatoes and set aside. Return the eggplant to the oven and roast for 25 to 35 minutes longer, until it's flattened out and uniformly soft. Cool until safe to handle. (The roasted vegetables can be covered and refrigerated for up to 2 days at this point.)

3. Reduce the oven temperature to 375°F.

4. To assemble the burger mixture, peel and chop the roasted eggplant (you should be able to pull the skin off with

your hands; it comes off in strips). Coarsely chop the roasted tomatoes. In a mixing bowl, combine the eggplant and tomatoes with the rice, onion, garlic, cilantro, curry powder, garam masala, molasses, salt, and cayenne. Fold in the mashed potato and potato starch. This is a somewhat loose mixture, so you won't be able to shape it into patties. Rather, divide it into 4 portions.

In an oven-safe skillet or nonstick sauté pan, heat the oil over medium-high heat. When hot, add the portions, pressing each gently with a spatula to form a round. Cook, turning once, until browned on each side, 6 to 10 minutes total. Transfer the pan to the oven and bake for 15 minutes, until the burgers are firm and cooked through.

▶ **PREP AND COOK TIME:** 1 hour
▶ **DO AHEAD:** Roast tomatoes and eggplant

4

TOFU, SEITAN, TEMPEH, AND TVP BURGERS

TOFU, SEITAN, TEMPEH, and textured vegetable protein (TVP) bring a boost of protein to any veggie burger. Even more so than beans, they are a blank canvas for you to take in any direction because they acquire the flavors of the ingredients they are paired with. They lend themselves particularly to Asian-inspired burgers, but when used correctly they can enhance almost any patty. Follow a few guidelines and you'll find them to be delicious base for all types of veggie burgers.

TOFU: Made from curdled soy milk, tofu is perhaps the most obvious choice of a protein base for veggie burgers. Because of its soft, spongy texture, it doubles as a primary protein and as a binder. I find that the biggest challenge when cooking with tofu is its texture. If too much is used in a burger, the tofu can sometimes fail to cook all the way through, and the resulting burger is heavy and dense and tastes raw. To avoid this, cut tofu into small pieces and bake or fry it before combining it with the other ingredients. This ensures that the final product will have a varied, fully seasoned texture. To further diversify the texture and to guarantee that the burgers will hold together without the use of other binders, purée half to three-quarters of the cooked tofu with the rest of the ingredients, and then fold into the remaining crumbled or chopped tofu.

To prepare tofu for cooking, you'll need to drain and dry it. If using firm or extra-firm tofu (which is recommended in these recipes), the tofu can be cut into thick slices, placed between a few layers of paper towels, and weighed down with something heavy, like a cutting board or a can of beans. More delicate types of tofu like soft and silken varieties should just be carefully blotted dry.

To store leftover tofu, cover with fresh water and keep in the refrigerator. If you change the water daily, it should last up to three or four days. You'll notice an off smell, somewhat sour like spoiled milk, when it has gone bad.

SEITAN: Seitan is the product of cooking wheat gluten, which is the primary protein found in many grains. There are plenty of decent premade brands on the market, both vacuum- and water-packed (and sometimes in cans, if you search your local Chinatown). But I think you'll discover that it's very easy to make on your own (see the Seitan Burger on page 197). Seitan has the dense, chewy texture of meat—this is what you're getting when you order "vegetarian duck" at a Chinese or Thai restaurant—and if prepared correctly, it can taste disarmingly similar.

My favorite way to cook seitan is to sauté it. It will brown on the edges, and whatever sauces you are cooking it in will caramelize on the exterior. In this chapter, in the Seitan Burger, it is literally used as a slab of protein slathered in barbecue sauce.

TEMPEH: Made from cultured, fermented soybeans, tempeh is often used to make vegan approximations of meat staples, such as veggie bacon and veggie sausage. It has a more robust nutritional profile and higher protein content than tofu, seitan, or TVP—its protein levels are similar to that found in many meats—and thus has a reserved space in the refrigerators of many vegetarians and vegans. Tempeh has a more pronounced, slightly nutty flavor than undressed tofu or seitan, and in my opinion it is one of the few soy products that can be enjoyed with minimal preparation.

Cooking tempeh removes the slightly sour taste it has when it is raw. In the recipes here, it is sautéed before being made into a burger, but it can also be steamed. Many prepared tempeh brands contain additional grains and seeds like wild rice and flax seeds. Be sure to select a variety that will complement the other ingredients in your burger.

TVP: Textured vegetable protein (TVP), which is simply dried soy flakes, has fallen out of favor in popular vegetarian cooking. On its own, it has the somewhat unpleasant flavor and texture of wet cardboard. But in veggie burgers it offers a protein boost, and when playing second fiddle to other vegetables and grains, such as in the Chipotle Black Bean Burgers (page 91), the texture gives a heft and chewiness that is otherwise hard to achieve in a veggie burger.

TVP needs to be reconstituted before it can be cooked. The ratio is *almost* 1:1; I have better results when about 1 tablespoon less water is used for every cup of TVP. TVP is very inexpensive and can be found at most stores that sell dry goods in bulk bins.

CHIPOTLE BLACK BEAN BURGER

CHIPOTLE BLACK BEAN BURGERS Ⓥ

THIS VEGAN BURGER makes a terrific breakfast when topped with scrambled tofu or a fried egg, slices of avocado, and a couple shakes of hot sauce. Or as a nontraditional spin, I also like to stuff it inside pita bread with salsa and a squeeze of lime, as pictured.

▶ **MAKES SIX 4-INCH BURGERS**

¾ cup textured vegetable protein (TVP)

⅔ cup boiling water

1½ cups cooked black beans

½ onion, roughly chopped

1 cup cooked brown rice

1 ear of corn, kernels sliced off with a knife, or ½ cup thawed frozen corn

¼ cup chopped cilantro

3 tablespoons all-purpose flour

3 chipotle chile peppers in adobo sauce, minced, plus 1 tablespoon sauce

Juice of 1 lime

1 teaspoon salt

¼ teaspoon dried chipotle pepper

¾ cup toasted bread crumbs

2 tablespoons oil

1. Place the TVP in a small bowl, pour over the boiling water, and let sit for 10 minutes.

2. Combine ½ cup of the black beans and the onion in a food processor and pulse until coarsely puréed. Place the remaining 1 cup beans in a bowl and coarsely mash with a potato masher or a fork. Fold in the reconstituted TVP, the bean-onion mixture, rice, corn, cilantro, flour, minced chipotle and its sauce, lime juice, salt, and dried chipotle. Fold in the bread crumbs. Let stand for 10 minutes so the crumbs can soak up as much moisture as possible. Shape into 6 patties.

3. In an oven-safe skillet or nonstick sauté pan, heat the oil over medium-high heat. When hot, add the patties and cook until browned on each side, 6 to 10 minutes total. Transfer the pan to the oven and bake for 12 to 15 minutes, until the burgers are firm and cooked through.

▶ **PREP AND COOK TIME:** 25 minutes

WATERCOURSE FOODS TEMPEH BURGERS Ⓥ ㉓

WATERCOURSE FOODS IN Denver, Colorado, has a veggie burger that is locally revered. Chef Rachel Kresley and manager Callie Liddell graciously offered their recipe, which uses tempeh to delicious effect. It is crumbled, sautéed with an assortment of vegetables, and then folded into wild rice. The arame was a surprise ingredient for me: A dried kelp seaweed that looks like black saffron threads, arame has a mild, slightly sweet flavor, and reconstitutes very quickly. It complements many types of dishes, particularly this veggie burger, and can be found in the Asian section of some grocery stores and at Asian markets.

▶ MAKES SIX 4-INCH BURGERS

½ cup wild rice

1 tablespoon olive oil

½ onion, diced

1 stalk celery, diced

1 carrot, diced

½ red bell pepper, diced

2 garlic cloves, minced

1 teaspoon dried parsley

½ teaspoon ground cumin

¼ teaspoon onion powder

¼ teaspoon garlic powder

¼ teaspoon ground fennel

1 teaspoon salt

¼ teaspoon freshly ground black pepper

1 (8-ounce) package tempeh (GF)

2 teaspoons fresh lemon juice

2 teaspoons soy sauce or tamari (GF)

2 teaspoons apple cider vinegar

1 teaspoon liquid smoke

½ teaspoon Worcestershire sauce (GF)

2 tablespoon arame, rehydrated according to package directions, drained, and chopped

1 tablespoon nutritional yeast

½ cup chickpea flour

1. Bring the rice and 1¼ cups water to a boil in a small saucepan. Reduce the heat, cover, and cook for 40 to 50 minutes, until the water is completely absorbed. Continue cooking for 10 minutes longer so as to overcook the rice; you want a mushy texture. Transfer to a baking sheet and cool completely.

2. Preheat the oven to 400°F. Line a baking sheet with parchment paper.

3. Heat the oil in a medium sauté pan over medium heat. Add the onion, celery, carrot, and red pepper and cook until softened, 6 to 8 minutes. Add the garlic, parsley, cumin, onion powder, garlic powder, fennel, salt, and black pepper. Crumble the tempeh over the vegetables. Sauté for 5 minutes over low heat. Add the lemon juice, soy sauce, vinegar, liquid smoke, and Worcestershire and deglaze, scraping up the browned bits with a wooden spoon. Cook until the liquid is fully absorbed, 3 to 5 minutes. Transfer to a mixing bowl and let sit until cool enough to handle. Add the rice, arame, and nutritional yeast, mixing with your hands.

4. Pulse half the mixture in a food processor until uniformly puréed. Return to the bowl with the remaining mixture and mix in the chickpea flour. The mixture will be dense and sticky. Shape into 6 patties and place on the prepared baking sheet.

5. Bake for 20 minutes, flipping the patties and rotating the pan halfway through, until firm and cooked through.

▶ PREP AND COOK TIME: 1 hour, 45 minutes, including cooling time

TOFU anD CHARD BURGERS Ⓥ

FEEL FREE TO substitute kale, beet greens, spinach, or any other dark leafy greens for the chard here. Puréeing half the cooked tofu is what gives this burger its structure; otherwise it splits apart in the pan.

▶ MAKES SIX 4-INCH BURGERS

8 ounces extra-firm tofu

4 tablespoons olive oil

1 bunch chard, cut into 1-inch pieces

3 tablespoons soy sauce or tamari (GF)

2 teaspoons agave nectar

2 teaspoons sesame oil

2 garlic cloves, minced

1 teaspoon grated fresh ginger

¾ cup toasted bread crumbs

Sweet Sesame Glaze (page 158)

1. Preheat the oven to 375°F.
2. Drain the tofu and cut into ½-inch slices. Layer the slices on half of a clean kitchen towel or a few layers of paper towels; fold over the other half of the towel or top with more paper towels. Set a broad, flat weight on top (a cutting board or plate with a can of beans placed on top) and let stand for about 10 minutes so as to squeeze out as much moisture as possible. Cut into ½-inch dice.
3. Heat 1 tablespoon of the oil in a skillet over medium heat. Add the chard and cook, tossing with tongs, until fully wilted, about 2 minutes. Transfer to a plate. When cool enough to handle, wrap in a clean kitchen cloth and squeeze out as much liquid as possible. Finely chop.
4. Wipe out the skillet and place over medium-high heat. Add 1 tablespoon oil, the soy sauce, agave nectar, and sesame oil, swirling the pan or stirring to combine. Add the tofu and cook, tossing occasionally, until much of the liquid is absorbed, about 12 minutes.
5. Purée half the tofu in a food processor. To the remaining tofu in the pan, add the chopped chard, garlic, and ginger and cook for 2 minutes. Transfer to a mixing bowl and coarsely mash with a potato masher. Fold in the puréed tofu. Fold in the

bread crumbs. Allow to stand for 5 to 10 minutes so that the crumbs soak up as much moisture as possible. Shape into 6 patties.

6. In an oven-safe skillet or nonstick sauté pan, heat the remaining 2 tablespoons oil over medium-high heat. When hot, add the patties and cook until browned on each side, 6

to 10 minutes total. Transfer the pan to the oven and bake for 12 to 15 minutes, until the burgers are firm and cooked through.

7. Drizzle with the sesame-honey glaze just before serving.

▶ PREP AND COOK TIME: 45 minutes

Seitan Burgers with Mango BBQ Sauce ⓥ

I HIGHLY RECOMMEND making your own seitan for this recipe. It's a much easier process than you'd expect, and there's plenty of room for improvisation, both in making the cooking broth as well as the seitan itself (see my variations below). The Mango Barbecue Sauce is also easy and delicious, but feel free to substitute your favorite barbecue sauce. Garnished with julienned cabbage, a handful of fresh cilantro, or scallions, and sesame seeds on a Pretzel Roll (page 119)—its salty forthrightness holds its own against the savory seitan—this burger really can't be beat.

▶ **MAKES SIX BURGERS**

COOKING LIQUID

1 tablespoon toasted sesame oil

1 small onion, roughly chopped

6 mushrooms, halved, or a handful of mushroom stems and scraps

1-inch piece fresh ginger, cut into thin slices

4 garlic cloves, crushed and peeled

3 stems fresh parsley

¼ cup soy sauce or tamari (GF)

SEITAN

1 cup vital wheat gluten

1 teaspoon ground ginger

1 teaspoon garlic powder

2 tablespoons soy sauce

1 teaspoon toasted sesame oil

BURGERS

1 tablespoon olive oil

1 cup Mango BBQ Sauce (page 159)

1. **PREPARE THE COOKING LIQUID:** In medium stockpot, heat the sesame oil over medium heat. Add the onion, mushrooms, ginger, garlic, and parsley, tossing to combine. Cover and cook for about 2 minutes, just until the onion begins to sweat and the parsley is a vibrant green. Add 6 cups water and the soy sauce. Bring to a boil, then reduce to a simmer. Partially cover and simmer for up to 2 hours, or until ready for the seitan.

2. **PREPARE THE SEITAN:** In a mixing

bowl, whisk together the vital wheat gluten, ginger, and garlic powder. In a separate bowl, combine ⅔ cup water, the soy sauce, and sesame oil. Add the wet ingredients to the dry, mixing with a wooden spoon until combined. It will be a fairly stiff, rubbery mixture. Don't worry if there's excess liquid in the bowl. Turn the mixture out onto a clean work surface and knead for 30 seconds. Let sit for 10 minutes, and then knead for another 30 seconds. With a dough scraper or knife, divide the dough into four sections. Gently stretch each piece with your hands until it resembles a cutlet.

3. Add the seitan pieces to the cooking broth. Cover the pot and simmer for 1 hour, turning the seitan every 15 minutes or so, until it is firm and has fully expanded. The seitan will expand *a lot*—add more water if necessary. Remove the pot from the heat and store the seitan in its cooking liquid until ready to use.

4. ASSEMBLE THE BURGERS: Drain the seitan thoroughly and squeeze some of the liquid out. Cut into 1-inch pieces. Heat the oil over medium-high heat in a large sauté pan or skillet. Add the seitan and sauté until browned, 8 to 10 minutes. Remove from the heat and add the barbecue sauce, tossing to combine. To serve, scoop the seitan mixture onto 6 rolls.

▶ PREP AND COOK TIME: 2 hours

NOTE: Seitan can be made in advance and kept in water or cooking liquid for 1 week in the refrigerator, or for up to 3 months in the freezer. If refrigerating, change the water daily.

▶ **Seitan Variations**

Homemade seitan is a blank slate for your culinary whims. The cooking broth can be plain water and the seitan nothing more than vital wheat gluten and water, or it can be an eclectic concoction. Let your imagination and curiosity run wild. Many vegan cooks recommend stirring ¼ cup nutritional yeast into the cooking broth for a rich enhancement.

Here are two variations:

■ ITALIAN-STYLE SEITAN: For the cooking broth, sauté 1 tablespoon tomato paste in 2 teaspoons oil until darkened. Add 6 crushed garlic cloves, 1 whole clove, 3 stems fresh parsley, a fresh sage leaf, and 10 peppercorns. Add 6 cups water. For the seitan, replace the dry spices with 1 teaspoon garlic powder, ¼ teaspoon dried sage, and ¼ teaspoon ground white pepper. Omit the sesame oil and soy sauce and increase the water to 1 cup.

■ SWEET-SPICY SEITAN: For the cooking broth, heat 2 teaspoons oil and sauté 4 roughly chopped scallions, 2 dried chile peppers, and 2 crushed garlic cloves. Add 6 cups water and 2 tablespoons agave nectar. For the seitan, replace the dry spices with 1 teaspoon ground all-spice and a pinch of cayenne. Omit the sesame oil and soy sauce and increase the water to 1 cup.

SMOKED TOFU BURGERS Ⓥ

SMOKED TOFU MAKES this burger reminiscent of the best barbecued foods. Top with grated raw carrot, a sprinkling of thinly sliced scallion, and a handful of fresh cilantro leaves.

▶ **MAKES SIX 4-INCH BURGERS**

3 tablespoons olive oil

1 medium onion, diced

1 (8-ounce) package smoked tofu, roughly diced

1 garlic clove, minced

1½ cups cooked black or red kidney beans

¼ cup minced cilantro

Juice of ½ lime

¼ teaspoon salt

Pinch of cayenne pepper

½ cup toasted bread crumbs

1. Preheat the oven to 375°F.
2. Heat 1 tablespoon of the oil in a medium sauté pan over medium heat. Add the onion and cook until translucent, 8 to 10 minutes. Add the tofu and cook until browned and slightly crisped, about 10 minutes. Stir in the garlic and cook until fragrant, 1 minute longer. Allow to cool slightly.
3. Transfer the tofu mixture to a food processor and add the beans, cilantro, lime juice, salt, and cayenne. Process until combined and slightly chunky. Transfer to a mixing bowl and fold in the bread crumbs. Adjust seasonings. Shape into 6 patties.
4. In an oven-safe skillet or nonstick sauté pan, heat the remaining 2 tablespoons oil over medium-high heat. When hot, add the patties and cook until browned on each side, 6 to 10 minutes total. Transfer the pan to the oven and bake for 12 to 15 minutes, until the burgers are firm and cooked through.

▶ **PREP AND COOK TIME:** 45 minutes

"GARDEN" BURGERS

THIS IS MY (improved) version of the Gardenburger found in the frozen aisle at the grocery store. Feel free to substitute yellow squash for the zucchini here, and you may want to experiment with other vegetables like grated carrots, broccoli florets, or chopped green beans.

▶ MAKES SIX 4-INCH BURGERS

1 medium zucchini, grated

1¼ teaspoons salt

½ cup textured vegetable protein (TVP)

⅓ cup hot water

3 tablespoons olive oil

1 medium onion, chopped

8 cremini mushrooms, thinly sliced

1 tablespoon tomato paste

2 tablespoons balsamic vinegar

1½ cups cooked chickpeas

2 eggs, beaten

1 cup cooked brown rice

2 tablespoons roughly chopped fresh parsley

¼ teaspoon ground black pepper

1 cup toasted bread crumbs

1. Preheat the oven to 375°F.

2. Toss the zucchini and ½ teaspoon of the salt in a colander and let sit for 10 minutes. Squeeze out as much liquid as possible.

3. Combine the TVP and hot water in a small bowl. Let stand for 10 minutes.

4. In a medium skillet, heat 1 tablespoon of the oil over medium heat. Add the onion and cook until it just begins to soften, about 5 minutes. Add the mushrooms and cook, stirring periodically, until softened and browned, 8 to 10 minutes. Add the tomato paste, quickly stirring to combine, and then the zucchini. Cook until the zucchini is slightly softened and dried out, 3 to 5 minutes. Add the vinegar and deglaze, scraping up browned bits with a wooden spoon or spatula. Remove from the heat and allow to cool slightly.

5. Combine the cooked vegetables, chickpeas, and eggs in a food processor and pulse until uniformly blitzed, though not completely puréed—you want the vegetables to be somewhat recognizable. Transfer to a mixing bowl and fold

in the reconstituted TVP, rice, parsley, pepper, and remaining ¾ teaspoon salt. Fold in the bread crumbs. Adjust seasonings. Shape into 6 patties.

1. In an oven-safe skillet or nonstick sauté pan, heat the remaining 2 tablespoons oil over medium-high heat. When hot, add the patties and cook until browned on each side, 6 to 10 minutes total. Transfer the pan to the oven and bake for 12 to 15 minutes, until the burgers are firm and cooked through.

▶ **PREP AND COOK TIME:** 30 minutes

GINGER-SOY TEMPEH BURGERS Ⓥ ⒼⒻ

THIS IS AN embarrassingly simple "burger"—marinated tempeh that's fried until crisp. In a whole-wheat roll, though, it's a marvelous base for fresh vegetables: lettuce, tomato, and thinly sliced red onion, of course, but also sprouts, avocado slices, and roasted red peppers.

▶ MAKES 4 BURGERS

2 packages (8 ounces each) tempeh (GF)

4 tablespoons olive oil

2-inch piece fresh ginger, peeled and thinly sliced

2 garlic cloves, crushed and peeled

2 sprigs fresh parsley

2 tablespoons soy sauce or tamari (GF)

1 teaspoon toasted sesame oil

2 teaspoons agave nectar or 1 tablespoon honey

¼ teaspoon black pepper

1. Slice the tempeh in half horizontally and cut each piece into two pieces.
2. Combine 3 tablespoons of the oil, the ginger, garlic, parsley, soy sauce, sesame oil, agave nectar, and pepper in a shallow baking pan. Add the tempeh, cover, and marinate for at least 1 hour, flipping every 15 minutes.
3. In a skillet or nonstick sauté pan, heat the remaining 1 tablespoon oil over medium-high heat. When hot, add the tempeh and drizzle with 1 tablespoon of the marinade. Cook until browned on the bottom, 5 to 7 minutes. Turn, drizzle with 1 tablespoon more of the marinade, and cook until browned on the other side, 5 to 7 minutes. Serve hot or at room temperature.

▶ PREP AND COOK TIME: 1 hour, 15 minutes, including time to marinate

▶ VARIATION: HAWAIIAN TEMPEH BURGER

Add ¼ cup pineapple juice to the marinade and replace the parsley with cilantro. After sautéing the tempeh, sauté slices of pineapple over high heat, until they begin to caramelize. Add them to the burgers with a handful of fresh cilantro leaves.

GINGER-SOY TEMPEH BURGER

5

BURGER BUNS

DECENT BURGER BUNS are available at all manner of grocery stores and bakeries, but it is a worthwhile treat (and perhaps a challenge) to make your own. If you don't own a stand mixer, don't let that stop you from trying out any of these recipes: bread has been around far, far longer than our precious KitchenAids. In fact, I often find that making breads and burger buns by hand gives me a better feel for the dough and results in a better outcome. Here are some guidelines.

A WETTER DOUGH WILL BE LESS DENSE: This realization, late in my life as a baker, shattered my approach to bread-making. I imagine that many of us who grew up helping make bread were told that we should be liberal with flour and then just knead, knead, knead, until the dough is "smooth and elastic." News flash: If you add too much flour, it will never get "smooth and elastic." One should, in fact, opt for a wetter dough and resist the urge to add additional flour during kneading; a dough that might stick a bit to your hands and the work surface will make better bread. This is one reason I've come to prefer making bread by hand to using a stand mixer: with the stand mixer, it's difficult to resist adding more flour as it sticks to the bowl and the dough hook.

To knead a slightly sticky dough, knead with one hand and hold a dough scraper in the other. Use the scraper to get underneath the dough and flip it after each kneading.

WHEN USING A STAND MIXER: If you do opt to use the stand mixer, here are a few guidelines: Start with the paddle attachment, which will ensure that the base dough is thoroughly combined. After about 2 minutes, switch to the dough hook. Add as much flour as is needed for the dough to form a ball. As the dough kneads, periodically turn off the mixer and remove the dough from the hook with your hands so that all the dough gets uniformly kneaded. I recommend kneading

by hand for the final few minutes, if for no other reason than posterity's sake.

COMBINING FLOURS: Breads and rolls that are not made entirely from all-purpose white flour have a more nuanced flavor and an enhanced nutritional profile. I prefer that half the flour be unbleached all-purpose white flour or bread flour, and the other half a combination of whole-wheat flour, oat flour, rye flour, and/or bran flour. Feel free to get creative. These types of flours can be purchased in small amounts at stores that sell dry goods in bulk. Be sure to store them in the refrigerator or freezer in an airtight container, where they will stay fresh for months.

SHAPING ROLLS: If you have a scale, divide the dough (which has been risen once) into 3-ounce portions. This is roughly the size of a large plum (fig. 1). Place a portion of dough on an unfloured surface. Place your dominant hand loosely, like a cage, around the dough with your fingers touching the surface of the table or countertop, then swirl the dough against the table in a circle (fig. 2). It should only take 10 to 15 seconds; the friction against the work surface causes the dough to collect at the base and shape itself into a ball (fig. 3).

1.

2.

3.

ALTERNATIVES TO HAMBURGER BUNS

ALL MY preaching in this chapter aside, there is no rule stating that veggie burgers must be served on burger buns. Veggie burgers are terrific served in pita bread, cold iceberg lettuce cups, mini ciabatta loaves, flour tortillas, between thick, toasted slices of fresh bread, or on top of a leftover piece of firm polenta, to name just a few examples.

Heidi Swanson, of 101cookbooks.com and the author of *Super Natural Cooking,* has a recipe for a veggie burger in her cookbook and on her Web site where the burger itself doubles as a bun: slice the cooked patty in half and sandwich your favorite fillings inside.

Of course, your burger need not necessarily be served in a bun or a bun-like medium. I enjoy eating veggie burgers on top of simple salads of mixed greens, or with breakfast as the base for a poached egg or scrambled tofu. Cold, leftover cooked veggie burgers are also perfect pocket foods, tasty completely unadorned.

BaSIC BURGER BUNS

HERE'S A SIMPLE recipe for homemade hamburger buns. The vegan alternatives (the rice milk, the agave nectar, and the vegan "eggwash") work beautifully. I always prefer a combination of wheat and white flours, but feel free to use all white. As with all burger buns, these are best toasted just before serving.

▶ **MAKES 10 BUNS**

1 cup warm milk or rice milk (110° to 115°F)

½ cup warm water (110° to 115°F)

2¼ teaspoons active dry yeast (1 package)

¼ cup olive oil, plus more for the dough bowl

1 tablespoon honey or 2 teaspoons agave nectar

2½ teaspoons salt

1½ to 2½ cups all-purpose flour

1 cup whole-wheat flour

½ cup oat flour

Eggwash: 1 beaten egg plus 1 tablespoon whole milk, or 2 tablespoons soy milk plus ½ teaspoon cornstarch

Poppy seeds, sesame seeds, wheat bran, flax seeds, or any combination

1. In a small bowl, stir together the warm milk and water. Whisk in the yeast and let stand for about 5 minutes, until the yeast begins to foam. Whisk in the oil and honey.

2. In a large bowl, whisk together 1 cup of the all-purpose flour, the whole-wheat flour, oat flour, and salt, and add the yeast mixture.

3. ■ IF MIXING BY HAND: Stir with a wooden spoon until thoroughly combined, adding more flour as needed, until it shapes into a ball. Turn the dough onto a floured surface and knead until smooth and elastic, 10 to 12 minutes, cautiously adding more flour as needed. Loosely shape the dough into a round.

   ■ IF USING THE STANDING MIXER: Begin with the paddle attachment, stirring the dough until combined, 2 minutes. Switch to the dough hook and knead until smooth and elastic, 8 to 10 minutes, cautiously adding more flour as needed. Loosely shape the dough into a round.

4. Pour 1 teaspoon or so oil into the mixing bowl and coat the dough with it. Cover with a piece of plastic wrap or a large tea cloth and let stand in a warm place until doubled in size, 1 to 2 hours.

5. Turn the dough onto a work surface and shape into 10 rolls.

6. Space the rolls 3 to 4 inches apart on a parchment-lined baking sheet. Cover again with plastic wrap or a tea towel. Let stand in a warm place until doubled in size, 1 to 2 hours.

7. Preheat the oven to 400°F.

8. Brush the buns with the eggwash and sprinkle with the seed garnish, being sure to cover the bun as much as possible. Bake for 15 to 18 minutes, turning the pan halfway through. Flip a roll over to check that it is browned on the base, which will indicate its doneness. Cool completely.

▶ PREP AND COOK TIME: 3 hours

BASIC BURGER BUNS

WHOLE-WHEAT BURGER BUNS

THESE BUNS HAVE the perfect burger bun texture: a crispy crust that yields to the soft goodness inside. The molasses gives them a slightly musky flavor and a dark brown color. I'm happy to eat them without anything sandwiched inside.

▶ MAKES 10 BUNS

1 cup warm water (110° to 115°F)

3 tablespoons warm whole milk (110° to 115°F)

2 tablespoons molasses

1 tablespoon sugar

2¼ teaspoons active dry yeast (1 package)

1 egg, beaten

1½ to 2½ cups bread flour

1 ¼ cups whole-wheat flour

4 teaspoons salt

2 tablespoons olive oil, plus more for the dough bowl

Eggwash: 1 beaten egg plus 1 tablespoon water or milk

Poppy seeds, sesame seeds, wheat bran, flaxseeds, or any combination thereof

1. In a small bowl, combine the warm water, milk, molasses, and sugar, whisking to combine. Whisk in the yeast and let stand for about 5 minutes, until the yeast begins to foam.

2. In a large bowl, whisk together 1 cup of the bread flour, the whole-wheat flour, and salt. Add the yeast mixture, oil, and egg.

3. ■ IF MIXING BY HAND: Stir with a wooden spoon until thoroughly combined, adding more flour as needed, until it shapes into a ball. Turn the dough onto a floured surface and knead until smooth and elastic, 10 to 12 minutes, cautiously adding more flour as needed. Loosely shape the dough into a round.

   ■ IF USING THE STANDING MIXER: Begin with the paddle attachment, stirring the dough until combined, 2 minutes. Switch to the dough hook and knead until smooth and elastic, 8 to 10 minutes, cautiously adding more flour as needed. Loosely shape the dough into a round.

4. Pour 1 teaspoon or so oil into the mixing bowl and coat the dough with it. Cover with a piece of plastic wrap or a large tea cloth and let stand in a warm place until doubled in size, 1 to 2 hours.

5. Turn the dough onto a work surface and shape into 10 rolls.

6. Space the rolls 3 to 4 inches apart on a parchment-lined baking sheet. Cover again with plastic wrap or a tea towel. Let stand in a warm place until doubled in size, 1 to 2 hours.

7. Preheat the oven to 400°F.

8. Brush the buns with the eggwash and sprinkle with the seed garnish, being sure to cover the buns as much as possible. Bake for 15 minutes, turning the pan halfway through. Flip a roll over to check that it is browned on the base, which will indicate its doneness. Cool completely.

▶ PREP AND COOK TIME: 3 hours

CORN BREAD BUNS

YEASTED CORN BREAD is a delicious alternative to corn bread that's leavened with baking soda or baking powder. It has a softer, spongier texture. Cornmeal is a heavier grain than flour, however, so the trick to getting these burgers right is to not overdo it with the flours. Additionally, these are more robust in flavor and texture than traditional hamburger buns, so they need to be paired with equally robust burgers, such as Sweet Potato Burgers with Lentils and Kale (page 79) or Best Portobello Burgers (page 57).

▶ **MAKES 10 BUNS**

½ cup warm milk (110° to 115°F)

½ cup warm water (110° to 115°F)

2¼ teaspoons active dry yeast (1 package)

¼ cup olive oil, plus more for the dough bowl

¼ cup honey or 2 tablespoons agave nectar

2 eggs

1 to 2 cups all-purpose flour

1 cup whole-wheat flour

1 cup cornmeal, plus more for sprinkling

2 teaspoons teaspoon salt

1½ cups fresh or thawed frozen corn

Eggwash: 1 beaten egg plus 1 tablespoon water or milk

Fleur de sel, for sprinkling

1. Whisk together the warm water and milk, and stir in the yeast. Let stand for about 5 minutes, until the yeast begins to foam. Whisk in the oil, honey, and eggs.

2. In a large bowl, whisk together 1 cup of the all-purpose flour, the whole-wheat flour, cornmeal, and salt. Add the yeast mixture.

3. ■ IF MIXING BY HAND: Stir with a wooden spoon until thoroughly combined, adding more flour as needed, until it shapes into a ball. Turn the dough onto a floured surface and knead until smooth and elastic, 10 to 12 minutes, cautiously adding more flour as needed. Loosely shape the dough into a round.

   ■ IF USING THE STANDING MIXER: Begin with the paddle attachment, stirring the dough until combined, 2 minutes. Switch to the dough hook and knead until smooth and elastic, 8 to 10 minutes, cautiously adding more flour as needed. Loosely shape the mixture into a round.

4. Pour 1 teaspoon or so oil into the mixing bowl and coat the dough with it. Cover with a piece of plastic wrap or a large tea cloth and let stand in a warm place until doubled in size, 1 to 2 hours.

5. Turn the dough onto a work surface and shape into 10 rolls.

6. Space the rolls 3 to 4 inches apart on a parchment-lined baking sheet. Cover again with plastic wrap or a tea towel. Let stand in a warm place until doubled in size, 1 to 2 hours.

7. Preheat the oven to 400°F.

8. Brush the buns with the eggwash and sprinkle with fleur de sel and a bit of large coarsely ground cornmeal. Bake for 12 to 15 minutes, turning the pan halfway through. Flip a roll over to check that it is browned on the base, which will indicate its doneness. Cool completely.

▶ **PREP AND COOK TIME:** 3 hours

PRETZEL ROLLS

THOUGH PRETZEL ROLLS are a minor ordeal and a mess to make, they are a true indulgence right out of the oven, one hand for the roll, the other for the squeeze-bottle of mustard. They're also delicious with hearty veggie burgers like the Seitan Burgers with Mango BBQ Sauce (page 97) and the Butternut Squash, Black Bean, and Chestnut Burgers (page 74).

▶ **MAKES 12 ROLLS**

¾ cup warm whole milk or rice milk (110° to 115°F)

¾ cup warm water (110° to 115°F)

2¼ teaspoons active dry yeast (1 package)

3 tablespoons olive oil, plus more for the dough bowl

3 to 3½ cups bread flour

1 teaspoon plus 1 tablespoon salt

¼ cup baking soda

Rock salt, for sprinkling

1. Combine the warm milk and water in a large bowl. Stir in the yeast and let stand for 5 minutes, until it bubbles and foams. Add the oil, 2½ cups of the flour, and 1 teaspoon of the salt.

2. ■ IF MIXING BY HAND: Stir with a wooden spoon until thoroughly combined, adding more flour as needed, until it shapes into a ball. Turn the dough onto a floured surface and knead until smooth and elastic, 10 to 12 minutes, cautiously adding more flour as needed. Loosely shape the dough into a round.

   ■ IF USING THE STANDING MIXER: Begin with the paddle attachment, stirring the dough until combined, 2 minutes. Switch to the dough hook and knead until smooth and elastic, 8 to 10 minutes, cautiously adding more flour as needed. Loosely shape the dough into a round.

3. Pour 1 teaspoon or so oil into the mixing bowl and coat the dough with it. Cover with a piece of plastic wrap or a large tea cloth and let stand in a warm place until doubled in size, 1 to 2 hours.

4. Turn the dough onto a work surface and shape into 12 rolls.

5. Space the rolls 3 to 4 inches apart

on a parchment-lined baking sheet. Cover again with plastic wrap or a tea towel. Let stand in a warm place until doubled in size, 1 to 2 hours.

6. Preheat the oven to 400°F. Meanwhile, fill a large pot with 4 to 5 inches of cold water and bring to a boil. Carefully add the baking soda (it will foam up) and the remaining 1 tablespoon salt.

7. After the rolls have risen a second time, add them to the boiling water in batches of four and poach 1 minute per side.

8. Place the poached rolls 1 inch apart on the parchment-lined baking sheet. With a sharp knife, draw an "X" on the top of each roll and sprinkle with the rock salt. Bake for 15 to 20 minutes, until dark brown all over. Transfer to a cooling rack.

▶ PREP AND COOK TIME: 3 hours

GLUTEN-FREE BURGER BREAD ⒼⒻ

A GLUTEN-FREE BURGER bun is a very difficult thing to get right! Most gluten-free doughs have the consistency of quick breads—you pour them into the pan rather than knead and shape them—such that it's virtually impossible to create a freestanding hamburger roll. My solution is to treat the buns as more of a cake or thick focaccia. Bake the batter in a 9x9-inch Pyrex baking dish or metal pan, let the bread cool, and then cut into 9 squares. The following recipe is adapted from Kelli and Peter Bronski's terrific cookbook, *Artisanal Gluten-Free Cooking,* which also has a fail-safe recipe for a gluten-free flour blend. But if you don't want to make your own, you can find prepackaged gluten-free flour blends at nearly every grocery store.

▶ **MAKES 9 ROLLS**

2¼ teaspoons active dry yeast (1 package)
2¼ cups warm whole milk (110° to 115°F)

1 tablespoon butter, melted, or olive oil
3 cups gluten-free flour blend
1 cup sorghum flour
1 teaspoon xanthan gum
2 tablespoons sugar
1½ teaspoons salt

1. Grease a 9×9-inch Pyrex baking dish or metal pan.
2. Stir the yeast into the warm milk and let stand for 5 minutes, until it bubbles and foams. Whisk in the melted butter.
3. In a mixing bowl, whisk together the flour blend, sorghum flour, xanthan gum, sugar, and salt. Stir in the yeast mixture. The batter will be very sticky. Spread the batter into the prepared baking dish. Cover and let rise for 1 hour.
4. Preheat the oven to 375°F.
5. Bake the bread for 30 to 35 minutes, until firm. Cool.
6. To serve, cut into 9 squares. Cut each square in half horizontally and fill with burgers and toppings.

▶ **PREP AND COOK TIME:** 1 hour, 45 minutes

SIDES: SaLaDS anD FRIES

One OF THE many pioneering aspects of vegetarian and vegan cooking is the rethinking of how a "proper" meal is supposed to be laid out. Growing up, I was taught that a meal was a big ol' hunk of meat taking up most of the plate, adorned with small amounts of starches and vegetables nudged up against the rim. Vegetarian and vegan eating has demonstrated, for me at least, that every aspect of the meal is equally important—whether it be salad, soup, side, or veggie burger. The sense of balance need not skew in one direction or another, and nothing needs to play second fiddle to anything else. To this end, I like to think of all the salads in this chapter as "mains"—even if they are "light" mains—rather than as secondary accompaniments.

That said, salads are extremely versatile dishes, and they don't have to be fussy. The best sides and salads, in my opinion, are often the simplest. Here are some suggestions for quick burger accompaniments if you are pressed for time:

* A plate of thickly sliced ripe tomatoes sprinkled with salt and pepper
* Quartered roasted beets
* Fresh arugula tossed with lemon zest and a simple vinaigrette
* A plate of crudités: florets of cauliflower and broccoli, asparagus spears, green beans, jícama slices, cherry tomatoes, and quartered cooked Red Bliss potatoes

And what would a burger cookbook be without fries? I offer a few different takes on oven-baked French fries (plus, I've included some guidelines for deep-frying for those special occasions when it's called for).

WATERMELON AND CITRUS SALAD ⓥ ⓖⒻ

MAKE THIS SALAD when watermelon is at its peak, sugar-sweet and juicy. I prefer basil to the fresh mint typically used in watermelon salad, but feel free to use mint instead.

▶ **MAKES 4 SERVINGS**

¼ cup fresh orange juice

Juice of 1 lime

1 tablespoon red wine vinegar

1 tablespoon Dijon mustard (GF)

1 shallot, minced

¼ teaspoon salt

¼ teaspoon ground white pepper

¼ cup grapeseed oil

2 oranges

6 cups 1-inch-cubed watermelon

¾ cup thinly sliced fresh basil

½ cup toasted slivered almonds

½ cup crumbled feta cheese (optional)

1. MAKE THE VINAIGRETTE: Combine the orange juice, lime juice, vinegar, mustard, shallot, salt, and pepper. Let stand for 10 minutes, then whisk in the oil. Adjust seasonings.

2. Slice off the top and bottom ends of the oranges and place the flat bottom on a cutting board. With a sharp chef's knife, cut off the peel in strips all the way around the orange, following the curve of the fruit. Slice the oranges into ¼-inch-thick rounds.

3. In a large bowl, toss the oranges and watermelon with the vinaigrette. Just before serving, garnish with the basil, almonds, and feta cheese if using.

▶ **PREP AND COOK TIME:** 20 minutes
▶ **DO AHEAD:** Cube watermelon, prepare vinaigrette

RED CABBAGE SLAW

RED CABBAGE SLAW GF

I MADE THIS salad at my friend Ilsa Jule's farm from basically everything I could get my hands on—a handful of thinly sliced fennel and fronds, some basil, grated carrots, and radishes. It was a fortifying, refreshing lunch in itself. The recipe below is a delicious simplification of that salad; feel free to improvise. If you can't find the thicker Greek-style yogurt, see page 163 for instructions on how to drain regular yogurt.

▶ **MAKES 4 SERVINGS**

½ head red cabbage
1 tablespoon rice wine vinegar
Salt
Freshly ground black pepper
3 tablespoons plain Greek-style yogurt
¼ cup coarsely chopped fresh dill

1. To julienne the cabbage: Quarter the cabbage along the core and with one flat side down, slice off the core in a diagonal swipe. With the broadest, flattest side down, slice the cabbage as thinly as possible—about ⅛ -inch-thick slices. Alternatively, julienne the cabbage using a mandoline.

2. Toss the cabbage with the vinegar and ½ teaspoon salt in a large bowl and let stand until it begins to wilt, 10 to 15 minutes. Pour off any excess liquid that has collected at the bottom of the bowl. Add the yogurt, dill, and pepper. Adjust seasonings. Serve.

▶ **VARIATION: ASIAN-STYLE SLAW**
Omit the yogurt and substitute the following dressing: 2 tablespoons soy sauce, 1 tablespoon honey, 1 teaspoon toasted sesame oil, 1 tablespoon toasted sesame seeds, and a few sliced scallions.

▶ **PREP AND COOK TIME:** 15 minutes

ROASTED CORN SALAD Ⓥ ⒼⒻ

THE CORN AND peppers for this easy summer salad can be cooked on the grill if you'd like: Heat the oil in a skillet directly on the grill, then add the peppers and corn and cook until tender.

▶ **MAKES 6 SERVINGS**

¼ cup olive oil

3 cups fresh corn (from about 6 ears)

2 jalapeño chile peppers, minced (seeded or not, depending on your personal heat threshold)

Juice of ½ lime

1 shallot, minced

Salt

Freshly ground black pepper

1. Preheat the oven to 350°F.
2. In an oven-safe skillet or sauté pan, heat the olive oil. Add the corn and peppers, tossing quickly to combine. Transfer the pan to the oven and roast, stirring occasionally, for 25 to 30 minutes, until the corn is tender. Let cool to room temperature.
3. In a large bowl, toss the corn and peppers with the lime juice, shallot, and salt and pepper to taste. Serve hot, chilled, or at room temperature.

▶ **PREP AND COOK TIME:** 30 minutes

ROASTED CORN SALAD

Raw Kale Salad
With Apples and Candied Walnuts Ⓥ ⒼⒻ

I LIKE THIS salad in the late fall, just when I begin to prepare myself for the oncoming winter and its dearth of fresh fruits and vegetables. It's delicious alongside almost any veggie burger, though the Sweet Potato Burgers with Lentils and Kale (page 79) and the Red Lentil and Celery Root Burgers (page 46) are top contenders for most-perfect matches.

▶ MAKES 6 SERVINGS

2 tablespoons sugar

¼ cup toasted walnuts, coarsely chopped

Pinch of dried thyme

Pinch of cayenne pepper

2 tablespoons soy sauce or tamari (GF)

1 tablespoon lemon juice

2 teaspoons honey or 1½ teaspoons agave nectar

1 teaspoon toasted sesame oil

¼ cup olive oil

1 bunch kale, cleaned and trimmed of stalks, and chopped or torn into ½- to 1-inch pieces

1 medium apple (a sweet and crisp one like Gala), cut into thin slices

½ cup shredded celery root

1. CARAMELIZE THE WALNUTS: Heat a dry, heavy-bottomed skillet over medium-low heat. Pour in the sugar and swirl the pan to distribute the sugar evenly. Cook, swirling the pan occasionally as the sugar begins to melt and brown. When it is a dark amber color, after 8 to 10 minutes, remove from the heat. Add the walnuts, thyme, and cayenne, tossing quickly so that everything is evenly coated. Turn onto a lightly greased plate or baking sheet to cool. Once cool, break into small pieces.

2. MAKE THE DRESSING: In a small bowl, combine the soy sauce, lemon juice, honey, and sesame oil. Whisk in the oil in a steady stream. Adjust seasonings.

3. In a large serving bowl, combine the walnuts, kale, apple, and celery root. Toss with the dressing just before serving.

▶ PREP AND COOK TIME: 25 minutes

▶ DO AHEAD: Caramelize walnuts

Beet, Pickle, and Apple Salad ⓥ ⓖⓕ

THE TRICK TO this embarrassingly simple salad is to use the right apple: it must be snappily crisp and tart. It will keep for 3 days in the refrigerator, though if you use red beets, most everything will have turned purple by then. This is an excellent use of leftover roasted beets.

▶ MAKES 4 SERVINGS

2 medium red or golden beets, scrubbed clean and trimmed of stems and fibrous roots

1 teaspoon olive oil

2 apples, such as Granny Smith or Cortland, peeled and cut into ¼-inch dice

1 cup Quick Pickles (page151), cut into ¼-inch dice

¼ cup coarsely chopped fresh mint

Freshly ground black pepper

1. ROAST THE BEETS: Preheat the oven to 400°F. Place the beets on a square of aluminum foil and rub with the olive oil. Wrap tightly in the foil and roast for 45 minutes to 1 hour, until they can be effortlessly pierced with a knife or skewer. Cool completely. When cool, peel the beets and cut into ¼ -inch dice.

2. Mix the beets with the apples, pickles, mint, and pepper to taste. Serve cold or at room temperature.

▶ PREP AND COOK TIME: 15 minutes to assemble, not including time to roast beets

▶ DO AHEAD: Roast the beets

**BLACK OLIVE AND ROASTED
POTATO SALAD WITH ARUGULA**

BLACK OLIVE AND ROASTED POTATO SALAD WITH ARUGULA Ⓥ ⒼⒻ

I LOVE A potato salad that is not mayo-based. The lemon, sherry vinegar, and arugula offset the briny-ness of the olive tapenade in this recipe. Feel free to substitute any variety of white potato you have lying around, but including the sweet potato is crucial.

▶ MAKES 4 SERVINGS

1 sweet potato (about 8 ounces)

6 fingerling potatoes or 1 large Yukon gold potato (about 8 ounces)

1 Red Bliss potato (about 8 ounces)

4 tablespoons black olive tapenade (see Note)

4 tablespoons olive oil

Juice of ½ lemon

1 tablespoon sherry vinegar

¼ teaspoon salt

½ red onion, halved and sliced into half-rings

3 cups loosely packed baby arugula

Freshly ground black pepper

1. Preheat the oven to 400°F.

2. Cut all of the potatoes into uniform 1-inch pieces (it's not necessary to peel them). Toss with 3 tablespoons of the tapenade and 2 tablespoons of the olive oil. Spread out on a baking sheet and roast for 30 to 35 minutes, until cooked through. Allow to cool.

3. In a large mixing bowl, whisk the remaining 1 tablespoon tapenade and 2 tablespoons olive oil with the lemon juice, vinegar, and salt. Add the red onion and let stand for 10 minutes. Add the potatoes and arugula and toss. Season with black pepper and serve immediately.

▶ PREP AND COOK TIME: 20 minutes
▶ DO AHEAD: Roast potatoes, make dressing

NOTE: Be sure to use a smooth tapenade rather than a chunky one, and one made from black olives, not green. Tapenade is very easy to make: Blitz 1 cup or so of your favorite pitted olives, thinned out with 2 tablespoons olive oil (or more, if needed), in a food processor.

Barley Salad with Beets and Goat Cheese

THIS SALAD IS the everyday version of the sensational Warm Farro Salad at Al Di La Trattoria in Brooklyn. It's delicious if you can pull off serving it warm. Here's how: Have everything ready to go—cook the beets and toast the hazelnuts, mix the dressing, have the cheese at room temperature—so that while the barley is still warm, you can rush it to the dinner table. I prefer to plate this salad individually so that the entire salad doesn't turn purple.

▶ MAKES 4 SERVINGS

2 medium beets, scrubbed clean and trimmed of stems and fibrous roots

1 teaspoon plus 3 tablespoons good-quality olive oil

¾ cup barley, rinsed

2 teaspoons sherry vinegar

½ teaspoon salt

Freshly ground black pepper

½ cup hazelnuts, toasted and coarsely chopped

2 tablespoons roughly chopped fresh tarragon, plus sprigs for garnish

4 ounces good-quality goat cheese

1. ROAST THE BEETS: Preheat the oven to 400°F. Place the beets on a square of aluminum foil and rub with 1 teaspoon of the olive oil. Wrap tightly in the foil and roast for 45 minutes to 1 hour, until completely tender. Cool completely. Peel the beets, quarter, and then slice into ¼-inch quarter-rings.

2. COOK THE BARLEY: Bring a large pot of salted water to boil. Add the barley and cook for 20 to 25 minutes, until tender. Drain and return to the cooking pot. Toss with the sherry vinegar. Cover the pot until ready to assemble the salad (this will keep the farro warm).

3. Whisk together the remaining 3 tablespoons olive oil, salt, and pepper. Toss with the barley, hazelnuts, and tarragon. Adjust seasonings.

4. Divide the barley mixture evenly among 4 salad plates, topping each with beets, goat cheese, and a sprig of tarragon.

▶ PREP AND COOK TIME: 1 hour, 30 minutes

▶ DO AHEAD: Roast beets, toast hazelnuts

CLASSIC BAKED FRIES ⓥ ⑤

I WASN'T A fan of baked French fries until I figured out this way to make them. It always seemed that the texture was wrong— overcooked on the outside, and dry and starchy like cotton on the inside. In this simple recipe, the combination of soaking the potatoes (which helps rid them of some excess starch—though as you'll find in the recipes for Cumin-Spiked Sweet Potato Fries [page 142] and Rutabaga Fries [page 145], you need *some* **starch), and then baking under a high heat solves the problem of texture.**

▶ **MAKES 4 SERVINGS**

3 large russet potatoes

3 tablespoons canola, vegetable, or grapeseed oil

Salt

1. Cut the potatoes into ¼-inch matchsticks (see direction). Cover with cold water in a large bowl and let stand for 30 minutes, or up to 12 hours in the refrigerator. When ready to cook, dry the fries as thoroughly as possible by running them through a salad spinner and then blotting with a towel.

2. Preheat the oven to 450°F. Lightly grease a large baking sheet.

3. Toss the potatoes with the oil and 1 teaspoon salt. Spread the potatoes on the prepared baking sheet. Bake, flipping every 10 minutes, for 30 to 40 minutes, until golden and crisp. Remove with a metal spatula and toss with additional salt to taste.

► Variations

Add different dried spices with the olive oil and salt before roasting the fries. Possibilities are endless, but here are a few suggestions:

- ■ 1 teaspoon smoked paprika
- ■ 1 teaspoon dried parsley, ½ teaspoon freshly ground black pepper, and ½ teaspoon dried oregano

- ■ 1 teaspoon ground cumin and 1 teaspoon hot or mild curry powder; after roasting, toss with 2 tablespoons chopped fresh cilantro

► **PREP AND COOK TIME:** 1 hour, including time for potatoes to soak

► **DO AHEAD:** Cut potatoes into matchsticks

CUTTING POTATOES INTO FRENCH FRIES

1. Make a single slice along the length of the potato so that it will stand flat on a cutting board (fig. 1).

2. Carefully slice lengthwise into broad, ¼-inch-thick discs (fig. 2).

3. Arrange 2 or 3 discs on top of each other and slice lengthwise into ¼-inch matchsticks (fig. 3).

TIPS:

- ■ Use a large, sturdy, sharp knife so that the knife, rather than your own elbow grease, will be doing the slicing.
- ■ Give yourself plenty of room on a large cutting board that won't slip around the countertop. Place a moist washcloth beneath the cutting board if yours is squiggling around.

STEP 1.

STEP 2.

STEP 3.

CUMIN-SPIKED ROASTED SWEET POTATO FRIES Ⓥ ⒼⒻ

UNLIKE RUSSET POTATOES, the secret to making crispy fries from sweet potatoes and other root vegetables is to *add* starch, rather than rinse it off. I opt for potato starch, which is tossed with the potatoes before the olive oil and salt. These fries are delicious dipped in Mango BBQ Sauce (page 159) or Almond-Yogurt Sauce (page 162). Omit the garam masala and cumin if you prefer basic sweet potato fries.

▶ **MAKES 4 SERVINGS**

3 large sweet potatoes
2 teaspoons potato starch or cornstarch
1½ teaspoons garam masala
1 teaspoon ground cumin
3 tablespoons olive oil
Salt

1. Preheat the oven to 450°F. Lightly grease a large baking sheet.
2. Scrub the potatoes clean and let dry. Cut into ¼-inch matchsticks (see page 140).
3. Combine the potato starch, garam masala, and cumin, and toss with the potatoes. Add the olive oil and 1 teaspoon salt and toss.
4. Spread the potatoes on the prepared baking sheet. Bake, flipping twice, for 25 to 30 minutes, until crispy on the outside and tender on the inside. Remove with a metal spatula and toss with additional salt to taste.

▶ **PREP AND COOK TIME:** 45 minutes
▶ **DO AHEAD:** Cut potatoes into matchsticks and keep covered with fresh water

DEEP-FRYING

DEEP-FRYING, WHICH involves completely submerging food in hot oil, may not be something you want to do frequently, but it is a worthwhile indulgence for celebrations and special occasions, and for when you can't think of any other way to console yourself.

To deep-fry, heat at least 4 inches of vegetable, peanut, or canola oil in a deep saucepan to 375°F. (Alternatively, heat the oil in a FryDaddy.) In batches, carefully lower the matchstick potatoes into the oil using a heat-safe slotted spoon or tongs. Avoid crowding the pan. Cook, stirring occasionally, for 8 to 10 minutes, maintaining the temperature, until the fries are golden brown and slightly puffed up. Transfer with a slotted spoon to a paper towel–lined baking sheet or a flattened paper bag to drain off excess oil. Salt, and serve immediately.

The oil can be cooled, strained, bottled, and reused for your next 3 or 4 deep-frying adventures. Be sure to dispose of it in accordance with your city's requirements—it should never be dumped down your sink's (or any other) drain. For information about correct disposal in your city, contact your local Department of Sanitation.

RUTaBaGa FRIES Ⓥ ⒼⒻ

UNLESS YOU LIVE in the South or shop in a store that carries a wide variety of somewhat less-familiar produce, rutabagas may be hard to come by. They are yellow-fleshed, slightly sweet, turnip-like root vegetables that have a waxy exterior (which is sometimes somewhat pink- or purple-hued). If you stumble upon some, be sure to try these fries.

▶ **MAKES 4 SERVINGS**

2 rutabagas
2 teaspoons potato starch or cornstarch
3 tablespoons olive oil
Salt

1. Preheat the oven to 450°F. Lightly grease a large baking sheet.
2. Slice off the top and bottom of the rutabagas so that they will rest flat on a cutting board. Then cut off the skin with a sharp paring knife or chef's knife by cutting against the curve of the flesh. (A vegetable peeler unfortunately doesn't cut thickly enough to scrape off all the skin.) Cut into ¼-inch matchsticks (see page 140).
3. Toss the potato starch with the rutabagas, then add the olive oil and 1 teaspoon salt.
4. Spread the rutabagas on the prepared baking sheet. Bake, flipping twice, for 25 to 30 minutes, until crispy on the outside and tender on the inside. Remove with a metal spatula and toss with additional salt to taste.

▶ **PREP AND COOK TIME:** 45 minutes
▶ **DO AHEAD:** Cut rutabagas into matchsticks and keep covered with fresh water
▶ **VARIATION: TURNIP FRIES**
Substitute 4 or 5 medium turnips for the rutabagas, but omit the potato starch; turnip fries are delicious, but they just won't crisp up as these do.

7

CONDIMENTS AND TOPPINGS

CONDIMENTS AND TOPPINGS are much more than an afterthought to a veggie burger, but as with side dishes, they need not be complicated or fussy. A bottle of Sriracha and a jar of mustard within reach may be all that is needed for a movie night, whereas you'll be willing to trouble yourself if you're cooking for a more elegant occasion.

I like to offer up the following (along with toasted burger buns) whenever I am serving veggie burgers:

* Thinly sliced tomato
* Thinly sliced red onion

* Crisp lettuce leaves, such as Bibb, romaine, red-leaf, or green-leaf
* Radish slices
* Cucumber slices
* Avocado slices
* Ketchup
* Mustard, whole-grain or Dijon
* Sriracha or other hot sauce
* Cheese (white Cheddar, Swiss, Gruyère) and vegan soy cheese

Here are some condiments that require a bit more advance planning:

* Caramelized onions (see Tuscan White Bean Burgers, page 32)
* Roasted garlic (see Tuscan White Bean Burgers, page 32), mashed into a spread

* Hummus
* Olive tapenade (see Note on page 135)
* Pesto: basil, mint, cilantro, or parsley, to name a few

The condiments and toppings included in this chapter show up regularly at my table. My Quick Pickles (page 151) are the easiest, most delicious pickles I've ever tasted; they never last very long. The Quick-Pickled Red Onions (page 155) are a snap to make as well and are a surprising, welcome addition to almost any veggie burger. And the Simple Yogurt Sauces (pages 161 and 162) make delicious spreads for the burgers as well as dipping sauces for crudités and French fries.

QUICK PICKLES

QUICK PICKLES Ⓥ ⒢

THESE PICKLES HAVE a clean flavor and are crisp—which is where so many other pickles fall short for me. Also, they are very easy. Make them when the farmers' market or your local grocer is overflowing with Kirbys.

▶ **MAKES 1 QUART**

4 Kirby cucumbers
½ cup cider vinegar
2 tablespoons kosher salt
2 tablespoons sugar
3 garlic cloves, crushed and peeled
1 teaspoon black peppercorns
1 teaspoon mustard seeds

1. Cut the cucumbers into whatever shape you please. I prefer ¼-inch-thick rounds cut on the bias.
2. Combine 2 cups water, the vinegar, salt, and sugar in a nonreactive bowl or jar that comes with a lid, stirring to dissolve. Add the cucumbers, ensuring that they are completely submerged. Cover the bowl or jar and let stand at room temperature overnight, or for 12 hours.
3. With a slotted spoon, transfer the cucumbers to a colander and rinse with cold water. Divide the cucumbers, garlic, peppercorns, and mustard seeds between 2 pint jars or place all in 1 quart jar. Pour the brine over, ensuring that the pickles are entirely submerged. Cover and chill for at least 2 hours. Can be kept, refrigerated, for about a month; the flavors of the garlic and other aromatics will be enhanced over time.

▶ **PREP AND COOK TIME:** 20 minutes, not including time to pickle and chill

▶ **VARIATIONS: OTHER AROMATICS**
- Add 2 sprigs of fresh thyme with the garlic, peppercorns, and mustard seeds.
- Omit the mustard seeds and add 1 dried chile pepper and 1 star anise with the garlic and peppercorns.
- Omit the mustard seeds and garlic; add 1 bay leaf, 1 sprig of thyme, and 1 cinnamon stick with the peppercorns.

FRIZZLED SHALLOTS Ⓥ ⒼⒻ

THESE CRISPY, SAVORY fried shallots are an unexpected but welcome addition to veggie burgers. I especially like them on Curried Eggplant and Tomato Burgers (page 85). In the absence of shallots, use a small white or red onion, sliced as thinly as possible.

▶ MAKES 1½ CUPS

8 shallots
Peanut, canola, or vegetable oil for frying
Salt

1. Peel the shallots and carefully slice them into ⅛-inch-thick rings. (If you have a mandoline, this is a good opportunity to use it.)

2. In a heavy-bottomed sauté pan or saucepan, heat a ½ inch oil over medium heat. Add the shallots and cook, stirring gently, for 8 or 10 minutes, until they begin to turn a golden-red color and turn crisp. Watch carefully, because once they begin to redden, they can easily brown and burn. Remove from the oil with a slotted spoon. Toss liberally with salt, and then drain on a few layers of paper towel or a flattened-out paper bag. Stored in an airtight container, the shallots will keep for up to 5 days.

▶ PREP AND COOK TIME: 15 minutes

QUICK-PICKLED RED ONIONS

QUICK-PICKLED RED ONIONS Ⓥ Ⓖⓕ

THIS STAPLE OF Mexican cuisine, a tempting snack on its own, is also a great addition to almost any burger, sandwich, or salad. Use any light vinegar you prefer: Champagne vinegar, red or white wine vinegar, plain white vinegar, rice vinegar, cider vinegar, or a combination thereof.

▶ MAKES 1½ CUPS

⅔ cup vinegar

3 tablespoons kosher salt

2 tablespoons sugar

1 large or 2 small red onions, sliced into ¼-inch-thick rings

1. In a bowl, combine 1 cup cold water, the vinegar, salt, and sugar, whisking to dissolve. Add the onions, ensuring that they are fully submerged. Let stand for at least 1 hour, or up to a week in the refrigerator, stored in the pickling liquid. Drain before serving.

▶ PREP AND COOK TIME: 15 minutes, not including time to pickle

CURRIED TOMATO RELISH Ⓥ ⒼⒻ

PAIR THIS RELISH with any curry spiced burger. It's a nice spin on pico de gallo and can be used to that effect on almost any of the burgers in this book.

▶ MAKES ½ CUP

1 cup cherry tomatoes

3 tablespoons minced cilantro

2 tablespoons finely minced red onion

Squeeze of fresh lime juice

1 teaspoon garam masala

½ teaspoon coriander

Salt

1. Preheat the oven to 450°F. Line a small baking sheet with foil.

2. Place the tomatoes on the prepared baking sheet. Roast for 20 minutes, stirring every 5 minutes, until they begin to shrivel or burst. Cool.

3. Coarsely chop the tomatoes and transfer to a mixing bowl. Add the cilantro, onion, lemon juice, garam masala, coriander, and salt to taste. Adjust seasonings. Stored in an airtight container in the refrigerator, the relish will keep for 4 to 5 days.

▶ PREP AND COOK TIME: 30 minutes, not including time to cool

POMEGRANATE-SESAME SAUCE Ⓥ ⓖⓕ

POMEGRANATE MOLASSES IS a
standard ingredient in Middle
Eastern cuisines. It's nothing
more than reduced pomegranate
syrup, and is delicious in sauces
and marinades and by itself as
a drizzle over ice cream and
oatmeal. It also shows up in the
Quinoa, Red Bean, and Walnut
Burger (page 45). It packs a
puckering punch in this recipe; a
little bit of the sauce goes a long
way. Many grocery stores now
carry pomegranate molasses,
but you may need to head to a
specialty store.

▶ MAKES ⅓ CUP

¼ cup pomegranate molasses
¼ cup soy sauce or tamari (GF)
1 tablespoon molasses
1 teaspoon sesame oil

1. Combine the pomegranate molasses, soy sauce, molasses, and sesame
oil in a small saucepan. Cook over
low heat, stirring occasionally, until
reduced by half, 6 to 8 minutes. It
will thicken as it cools. This sauce
will keep for up to 2 weeks in the
refrigerator.

▶ PREP AND COOK TIME: 10 minutes,
not including time to cool

sweet sesame glaze ⓥ ⓖⒻ

USE THIS GLAZE as a base for pan-fried tofu or a stir-fry sauce. It's brightened up with a touch of pomegranate molasses, and the honey lends a surprising savory depth.

▶ MAKES ½ CUP

½ cup soy sauce or tamari (GF)

1 tablespoon toasted sesame oil

2 teaspoons agave nectar or 1 tablespoon honey

½ teaspoon pomegranate molasses

2 tablespoons sesame seeds

2 tablespoons thinly sliced scallions (including 1 inch of the dark green parts)

1. Combine the soy sauce, sesame oil, honey, and pomegranate molasses in a small saucepan and cook over medium heat, swirling the pan often, until slightly reduced, about 5 minutes. Remove from the heat, stir in the sesame seeds, and allow to cool to room temperature; it will thicken slightly as it cools. The sauce will keep in an airtight container in the refrigerator for up to 3 days. Stir in the scallions just before serving.

▶ **PREP AND COOK TIME:** 10 minutes, not including time to cool

MANGO BBQ Sauce Ⓥ ⒼⒻ

THIS IS A great everyday barbecue sauce for all kinds of burgers. It also works well as a dipping sauce for French fries. If you'd like, amp up the heat by adding a bit more cayenne and chili powder. The flavors improve after a day or two, so it's best to make it in advance.

▶ MAKES 2 CUPS

1 cup ketchup (GF)

¾ cup mango chutney

½ cup plus 1 tablespoon cider vinegar

2 teaspoons Dijon mustard (GF)

1 teaspoon chili powder

1 teaspoon liquid smoke

1 teaspoon molasses

2 garlic cloves, minced

¼ teaspoon cayenne pepper

1. Combine all the ingredients in a medium saucepan. Bring to a boil, reduce to medium, and cook until slightly reduced and thickened, 30 to 40 minutes.

2. Transfer to a food processor or blender and purée. Alternatively, purée with an immersion blender. Allow to cool, and then refrigerate until ready to use. The sauce will keep in an airtight container in the refrigerator for up to 5 days.

▶ PREP AND COOK TIME: 1 hour

FOUR SIMPLE YOGURT SAUCES GF

PLAIN YOGURT IS a refreshing base for any number of savory and sweet sauces, particularly as an alternate to mayo-based sauces. I prefer Greek-style drained yogurt because it doesn't split from the whey when left to sit, and also because of its rich, luxuriant texture, but these recipes are equally delicious with undrained yogurt, which you can drain yourself if you please (see direction). All these recipes work both as spreads for burgers and sandwiches and dipping sauces for chips and fries. The sauces can be made a few hours in advance. The whey may separate, in which case just stir until combined and smooth.

CUCUMBER-YOGURT SAUCE GF
▶ MAKES 1¼ CUPS

½ red onion, minced

2 teaspoons lemon juice

½ teaspoon salt

1 small cucumber, grated or finely chopped

1 cup Greek-style plain yogurt

¼ cup loosely packed chopped fresh mint

1 garlic clove, minced

Pinch of cayenne pepper

1. Combine the onion, lemon juice, and salt in a medium bowl and let stand for a few minutes (while you grate or finely chop the cucumber). Add the cucumber, yogurt, mint, garlic, and cayenne. Adjust seasonings.

CURRIED YOGURT SAUCE GF
▶ MAKES 1 CUP

1 cup Greek-style plain yogurt

2 tablespoons finely minced cilantro

2 teaspoons lime juice

2 teaspoons curry powder

1 teaspoon coriander

½ teaspoon salt

Pinch of cayenne pepper

Pinch of sugar or drizzle of honey

1. Combine all the ingredients. Adjust seasonings.

ALMOND-YOGURT SAUCE GF
▶ MAKES 1¼ CUPS

¾ cup Greek-style plain yogurt

½ cup almond butter

2 tablespoons finely minced fresh parsley

1 teaspoon ground cardamom

½ teaspoon honey

¼ teaspoon salt

1. Combine all the ingredients. Adjust seasonings.

▶ PREP AND COOK TIME: 10 minutes

TAHINI-YOGURT SAUCE GF
▶ MAKES 1¼ CUPS

¾ cup Greek-style plain yogurt

½ cup tahini

2 tablespoons finely minced fresh parsley

1 garlic clove, minced

1 teaspoon lemon juice

½ teaspoon ground cumin

¼ teaspoon salt

Dash hot sauce

1. Combine all the ingredients. Adjust seasonings.

DRAin YOUR OWn YOGURT

IF YOU can't find Greek-style yogurt, it's very easy to drain plain yogurt yourself in order to achieve the thickness that is the hallmark of the Greek style. Some yogurts have added gelatins and emulsifiers that prevent the whey from separating; you'll need to make sure to use a yogurt that does not include these. Stir the yogurt until smooth, and then scoop it into a triple layer of cheesecloth. Tie the corners of the cheesecloth around a wooden spoon or other long, sturdy utensil. Balance the spoon across the rim of a tall, deep bowl so that the yogurt is fully suspended and the whey can drip into the bowl. Allow to drain for 30 to 45 minutes, until desired thickness is reached. To make yogurt cheese, allow the yogurt to drain overnight in the refrigerator.

ACKNOWLEDGMENTS

First and foremost, thank you Matthew Lore, the publisher, editor, and my friend, who had the idea for this cookbook, trusted that I was capable of executing it, and has been crucial at every stage of the process.

Thank you to my family: My brother and his wife, Max and Casady Volger, my grandfather, Glen Scott, and especially my dad, Ron Volger, my first editor, whose kitchen got a workout during the photo shoots. I am lucky to have such a supportive family.

Thank you to friends, tasters, recipe testers, and voices of encouragement: Meghan Best, Lesley Enston, Izzy Forman, Katie Gilligan, Emily Gould, Kathryn Hunt, Ilsa Jule, Arch Noble, Ann Pappert, and Brian Ulicky.

Thank you to Christina Heaston for her beautiful photographs; Sean Dougherty for terrific last-minute photos; the breathtakingly thorough copyeditor Deri Reed; and Pauline Neuwirth for her gorgeous book design.

Thank you to my colleagues over the course of writing this book: James Atlas, Lauren LeBlanc, Nataša Lekić, Peter Desrochers, and the rapidly expanding team at Atlas & Co.; Chef Pascal Bonhomme, Lottie Baglan, and everyone at Pascalou (and special thanks to Chef Pascal for recipe ideas and fielding food questions).

A final and important thank-you to Matt Rebula, who tasted almost as many veggie burgers as I did, washed as many of the correlating dishes, helped with midnight-hour edits, and continues to make everything more fulfilling and fun.

The following cookbooks have been very helpful
sources of inspiration and information:

Bronski, Kelli, and Peter Bronski. *Artisanal Gluten-Free Cooking*. New York: The Experiment, 2009.

Dornenburg, Andrew, and Karen Page. *The Flavor Bible*. New York: Little, Brown, 2008.

Jaffrey, Madhur. *Madhur Jaffrey's World Vegetarian*. New York: Clarkson Potter, 2002.

Madison, Deborah. *Vegetarian Cooking for Everyone*. New York: Broadway Books, 1997.

Moskowitz, Isa Chandra. *Vegan with a Vengeance*. New York: Marlowe & Company, 2005.

Moskowitz, Isa Chandra, and Terry Hope Romero. *Veganomicon*. New York: Da Capo, 2007.

Swanson, Heidi. *Super Natural Cooking*. Berkeley, CA: Celestial Arts, 2007.

A

almond meal, 80
    in sweet potato burgers, 79–80
Almond-Yogurt Sauce, **160,** 162
apples
    in edamame burgers, 28–29
    raw kale salad with, 130, **131**
    in salad with beets and pickles, 132
Arborio rice, 8
Armenian Lentil Burgers, 24, **25,** 26
Arugula, Black Olive and Roasted Potato Salad
    with, **134,** 135
Asian-Style Slaw, 127

B

baking veggie burgers, 15–16
Barley, Mushroom Burgers with, 64, **65**
Barley Salad with Beets and Goat Cheese, 136,
    137
beans, 2–6, 19–20. *See also* black beans;
    chickpeas; lentils; red beans
    bean burgers, **22,** 23
    edamame burgers, 28–29
    Fava Bean Burgers, 42, **43**
    Tuscan White Bean Burgers, 32, **33**
Beet, Pickle, and Apple Salad, 132
Beet and Brown Rice Burgers, 59–60, **60**
beets, 55
    in barley salad, 136, **137**
    Beet "Tartare," 66, **67**
black beans
    in bean burgers, 23
    beet and brown rice burgers, 59–60
    butternut squash and chestnut burgers,
        74–75

chipotle burgers, **90,** 91
    in pub grub burgers, 51
    in Smoked Tofu Burgers, 101
Black Olive and Roasted Potato Salad with
    Arugula, **134,** 135
black pepper, 27
blanching greens, 54
boiling beets or squash, 55
bread. *See* burger buns
bread crumbs, 9–11
brown basmati rice, 7–8. *See also* rice
Bulgur, Cashew-Leek Burgers with Lentils and,
    38, 39–40
burger buns, 107–8
    alternatives, 110
    basic buns, 111–12, **113**
    corn bread, 117–18
    gluten-free, 122
    Pretzel Rolls, 119–20, **121**
    shaping, 108, **109**
    whole-wheat, **114,** 115–16
Butternut Squash, Black Bean, and Chestnut
    Burgers, 74–75

C

cabbage slaws, **126,** 127
cannellini beans, 20
caramelized onions, 32
Carrot Burgers, Thai, 61–62, **63**
Cashew-Leek Burgers with Bulgur and Lentils,
    38, 39–40
cast-iron skillets, 14
Cauliflower Burgers, Baked, 71–72, **73**
Celery Root and Red Lentil Burgers, 46, **47,** 48
celiac disease, 11

chard, 54
    Tofu and Chard Burgers, **94,** 95–96
Cheese, Stuffed Portobello Burgers with, 58
Cheese and Spinach Portobello Burgers, 58
chestnuts, 75
    butternut squash burgers with, 74–75
chickpeas, 20
    in bean burgers, 23
    falafel burgers, **34,** 35–36
    in Fava Bean Burgers, 42, **43**
    in "Garden" Burgers, 103–4
    in pub grub burgers, 51
    Spinach-Chickpea Burgers, **76,** 77–78
chile peppers
    Chipotle Black Bean Burgers, **90,** 91
    in Roasted Corn Salad, 128
    in Thai Carrot Burgers, 61–62
Citrus and Watermelon Salad, 125
condiments and toppings, 147–48
    Curried Tomato Relish, 156
    Frizzled Shallots, 152, **153**
    Mango BBQ Sauce, 159
    pickles, **150,** 151, **154,** 155
    Pomegranate-Sesame Sauce, 157
    Sweet Sesame Glaze, 158
    yogurt sauces, **160,** 161–62
cooking equipment, 13–15
cooking methods, 15–17
Cooks Illustrated, 39
Corn Bread Buns, 117–18
Corn Burgers with Sun-Dried Tomatoes and
    Goat Cheese, **82,** 83
Corn Salad, Roasted, 128, **129**
cucumbers, pickled, **150,** 151
Cucumber-Yogurt Sauce, **160,** 161
Cumin-Spiked Roasted Sweet Potato Fries, 142
curries
    eggplant and tomato burgers, **84,** 85–86
    sweet potato burgers, 79–80
    tomato relish, 156
    yogurt sauce, **160,** 162

D

dough scraper, 108
dried beans, 2, 4, 6

E

edamame, 20
    burgers, 28–29
Eggplant and Tomato Burgers, Curried, **84,**
    85–86
egg replacer, 12–13
egg substitutes, 11–13
Ener-G Egg Replacer, 13
epazote, 4

F

Falafel Burgers, Baked, **34,** 35–36
Fava Bean Burgers, 42, **43**
flaxseed, 12
flour, making your own, 10
flour for burger buns, 108
food processors, 13–14
fries
    baked, **138,** 139
    cutting the potatoes, 140, **141**
    deep fried, 143
    rutabagas, 145
    sweet potatoes, 142
    turnips, 145
    variations, 140
Frizzled Shallots, 152, **153**
frying, 15–16, 36, 143

G

garbanzo beans. *See* chickpeas
"Garden" Burgers, **102,** 103–4
garlic, roasting, 32
gluten-free bread crumbs, 10
Gluten-Free Burger Bread, 122
gluten-free diet, 10
goat cheese
    barley salad with beets and, 136, **137**

in Beet "Tartare," 66
corn burgers with sun-dried tomatoes
and, **82**, 83
grains, 7–8. *See also* rice
quinoa burgers, **44**, 45, 49
Great Northern beans, 20
greens, 54. *See also* kale; spinach
in Tofu Burger variations, 95–96
grilling, 16–17, 57

H

Hawaiian Tempeh Burgers, 105
hazelnuts, in Barley Salad with Beets and Goat
Cheese, 136, **137**
heirloom beans, in bean burgers, 23
herbs, 30–31

I

infused oils, 31
Italian-Style Seitan, 99–100

K

Kalamata olives, in Tuscan White Bean
Burgers, 32–33
kale, 54
salad with apples and candied walnuts,
130, **131**
sweet potato burgers with, 79–80, **81**
kidney beans, 20. *See also* red beans

L

leeks, 41
and cashew burgers, **38**, 39–40
leftovers, 17–18
legumes. *See* beans
lentils, 20
Armenian burgers, 24, **25**, 26
cashew-leek burgers with, **38**, 39–40
red lentil burgers, 46, **47**, 48
sweet potato burgers with, 79–80, **81**

M

malt, 11
Mango BBQ Sauce, 159
seitan burgers with, 97, **98**, 99
meat grinders, 14
miso paste, in Portobello Burgers, 57–58
mushrooms, 55–56
in cashew-leek burgers, 39–40
in "Garden" Burgers, 103–4
Mushroom Burgers with Barley, 64, **65**
portobello burgers, 57–58, 69–70

N

navy beans, 20
nuts. *See also* walnuts
in barley salad, 136, **137**
cashew-leek burgers, **38**, 39–40

O

oil for cooking, 17
olive oil for herb infusions, 31
olive tapenade, 135
onions, caramelizing, 32
organic foods, 2

P

panfrying veggie burgers, 15–16
panko bread crumbs, 10
pickles, 132, **150**, 151, **154**, 155
Pomegranate-Sesame Sauce, 157
Portobello Burgers
tortilla-crusted stuffed, 69–70
with variations, 57–58
potatoes, 11–12
baked fries, **138**, 139
cutting into French fries, 140, **141**
deep fried, 143
potato salad, roasted, **134**, 135
potato mashers, 14
potato starch, 11–12
presoaking, 4–5, 7–8

Pretzel Rolls, 119–20, **121**
Pub Grub Veggie Burgers, **50,** 51

Q

Quick-Pickled Red Onions, **154,** 155
Quick Pickles, **150,** 151
    in Beet, Pickle, and Apple Salad, 132
    variations, 151
Quinoa, Red Bean, and Walnut Burgers, **44,**
    45
Quinoa Burgers, Baked, 49

R

red beans
    in bean burgers, 23
    in Beet and Brown Rice Burgers, 59–60
    Quinoa, Red Bean, and Walnut Burgers,
        44, 45
    in Smoked Tofu Burgers, 101
Red Cabbage Slaw, **126,** 127
Red Lentil and Celery Root Burgers, 46, **47,** 48
red onions, pickled, **154,** 155
resources, 167
rice, 7–8
    beet and rice burgers, 59, **60**
    in black bean burgers, 91
    in edamame burgers, 28–29
    in eggplant and tomato burgers, 85–86
    in "Garden" Burgers, 103–4
Roasted Corn Salad, 128, **129**
roasting
    beets, 55
    garlic, 32
    mushrooms, 56, 69
    spices, 27
    squash, 55
Romanesco Burgers, Baked, 72
Rutabaga Fries, 145

S

salads, 123–24

Asian-Style Slaw, 127
barley with beets and goat cheese, 136,
    137
Beet, Pickle, and Apple Salad, 132
kale salad, raw, 130, **131**
Red Cabbage Slaw, **126,** 127
Roasted Corn Salad, 128, **129**
roasted potato salad, **134,** 135
Watermelon and Citrus Salad, 125
salad spinners, 13
salt, adding to beans, 6
sautéing, 54, 56
sauté pans, 14
seaweed
    in portobello burgers, 58
    in Tempeh Burgers, 92–93
Seeded Edamame Burgers with Brown Rice
    and Apples, 28–29
seitan, 12, 88
    burgers with BBQ sauce, 97, **98,** 99
    Italian-style, 99–100
    sweet-spicy, 100
Sesame Glaze, Sweet, 158
Sesame Seaweed Portobello Burgers, 58
Shallots, Frizzled, 152, **153**
shaping burger buns, 108, **109**
shaping burgers, 15
side dishes, 123–24. *See also* fries; salads
sieves, 13
"sliders," 17
Smoked Tofu Burgers, 101
soaking beans, 4
soy products, 20, 87–89. *See also* edamame;
    tempeh; tofu; TVP
spices, 27
spinach, 54
    in butternut squash burgers, 74–75
    chickpea burgers, **76,** 77–78
    portobello burgers, 58
    in quinoa burgers, 49
squash, 54–55

steaming
    beets, 55
    greens, 54
    potatoes, 12
    rice, 7–8
storing cooked beans, 6
Stuffed Portobello Burgers, 58, 69–70
Sun-Dried Tomatoes, Corn Burgers with Goat
    Cheese and, **82,** 83
sweet potatoes
    burgers with lentils and kale, 79–80, **81**
    fries, 142
    in roasted potato salad, **134,** 135
Sweet Sesame Glaze, 158
Sweet-Spicy Seitan, 100

T

Tahini-Yogurt Sauce, **160,** 162
tempeh, 88–89
    ginger-soy burgers, 105, **106**
    Hawaiian burgers, 105
    Tempeh Burgers, 92–93
Thai Carrot Burgers, 61–62, **63**
tofu, 87–88
    Smoked Tofu Burgers, 101
    Tofu and Chard Burgers, **94,** 95–96
Tomato and Eggplant Burgers, Curried, **84,**
    85–86
Tomatoes, Sun-Dried, Corn Burgers with Goat
    Cheese and, **82,** 83
toppings. *See* condiments and toppings
Tortilla-Crusted Stuffed Portobello Burgers,
    69–70
Turnip Fries, 145
turtle beans. *See* black beans
Tuscan White Bean Burgers, 32, **33**
TVP (textured vegetable protein), 88–89
    in black bean burgers, 91
    in "Garden" Burgers, 103–4

V

vegetables, cooking, 53–56

W

walnuts
    in Fava Bean Burgers, 42, **43**
    kale salad with candied walnuts, 130, **131**
    quinoa and red bean burgers, **44,** 45
Watercourse Foods, Denver, 92
Watermelon and Citrus Salad, 125
wheat allergy, 11
wheat byproducts, 11
wheat-free bread crumbs, 10
wheat-free diet, 11
wheat gluten, 12. *See also* seitan
    in butternut squash burgers, 74–75
white beans, 20
    Tuscan White Bean Burgers, 32, **33**
Whole-Wheat Burger Buns, **114,** 115–16

Y

yogurt, draining, 163
yogurt sauces, **160,** 161–62
Yukon Gold potatoes, 12, 85, 135